My Dad,

or Why Did God Choose Me?

My Dad,

or Why Did God Choose Me?

Jim O'Farrell Jr.

iUniverse, Inc.

New York Lincoln Shanghai

My Dad, or Why Did God Choose Me?

iUniverse books may be ordered through booksellers or by contacting:

iUniverse
2021 Pine Lake Road, Suite 100
Lincoln, NE 68512
www.iuniverse.com
1-800-Authors (1-800-288-4677)

ISBN-13: 978-0-595-38442-6 (pbk)
ISBN-13: 978-0-595-82820-3 (ebk)
ISBN-10: 0-595-38442-0 (pbk)
ISBN-10: 0-595-82820-5 (ebk)

Printed in the United States of America

Acknowledgement

After I suggested this book to Dad, Maria O'Farrell volunteered to be our guiding light. Without her force and work the book would never have been finished.

Dad often told me the Queen of England liked to hang around him.
Now I believe it!

Contents

Introduction xi

Prologue 1

Dad's Tale 5

    Includes:

- Rocky Marciano
- Mario Cuomo
- Joe Louis
- Jack Newfield
- "Maria" of *Sesame Street*
- George Foreman
- Wendy Barrie
- Emile Griffith
- Gil Clancy, T.V. Commentator
- David Lerner

Epilogue: An Open Letter to My Son 97

A Son's Tale (Me) 99

My Sister's Tale—Anne Marie 111

The Final Curtain 127

About the Author 129

Introduction

My Dad, sister and I are a triangle. We range from racehorse owner in New York, to University of Arizona worker in Tucson, (that's me), and multi-state play producer located in Long Island, that's Anne Marie, my older sister.

We are diverse in locale, diverse in hobbies, and similar in temperament. I don't know what keeps a functional family from becoming dysfunctional. Maybe it's in the genes, but I doubt it.

I haven't studied this, nor have I read in depth on it. I've pondered, as so many others have, and I've read the psychobabble current in magazines and books. So many theories and so little sense. May I hazard a guess that we will never really know in our lifetimes.

Although I have titled the book *My Dad* or *Why Did God Choose Me*, it's all in fun, but there may be lessons in our three stories that have seeds of similarity, which can contribute to some understanding of function and dysfunction. There are three of us now, and none is like the other in behavior or thinking. I'm sure this is true in so many families. But how may times have you heard the phrase "he (or she) is just like his father (or mother)." Or similarly, brothers are just like their sisters, or other brothers, and or sisters.

You also hear quite the opposite, such as "He or she is so different from the rest of the family." This is the trap that analysts and theoreticians are confronted with in their exploration of human activity.

One hundred years from now some extraordinarily bright psychobabblist will quietly turn to a friend, look about him lest someone will hear, and say, "How the hell do I know."

These are the tales and musings of a family that is tangentially similar, yet equally diverse in actions and beliefs. Dad was an influence, but not a commander. My father, although rarely available, has always been the glue. His sense of right and wrong permeated the house like a blazing fire, and we were unable to escape, thank God. Deep in our psyche was buried the thought, "I wonder what Daddy would think."

He held a loose rein and occasionally we went ahead and broke a rule. We didn't realize at the time he probably knew what we were doing. As we grew older he knew we needed no reins, and we were our own selves. He has almost let go completely. He knows we have respect. Respect for ourselves, and respect for others, for we have been imbued with this quality as a necessity, as much a necessity as eating and sleeping and living.

This may have come from his DNA. If it has he has successfully passed it on to us.

Thanks Daddy.

P.S. I've asked my Pop to begin the book by telling us his version of his life, and his time with us. I dragged my sister in also.

Prologue

As Jim's father I asked permission to write a prologue to his book. Strange asking your son's permission, but what the hell, times change.

Thinking back upon the days when I was father to a teen-age daughter, Anne Marie, and a four year younger son, Jimmy, I am forced to reflect upon the question…was I a good Dad or a bad Dad, or a somewhere in-between Dad. I'm on my side, so I'll choose the former, knowing that I really have no idea.

I'm sure every father in America has asked himself that very question, although, if they haven't, they should have.

Motherhood is even more exasperating, as the children expect even more from the mother, and many Moms today have jobs to worry about. Younger children are either at home with a nanny, called a baby-sitter in the past, or deposited at a commercial sit-in, for the most part a well-established and successful pre-kindergarten mad house.

All this lifts some of the burden of fathering from the male of the house, consequently eliminating eight or nine hours from his paternal duties. Chances are the first few hours at home Dad is met with overwhelming joy and he becomes a part-time hero. Mom watches and wonders, though usually with happy equanimity. Of course, I am talking about a functioning family.

A dysfunctional family's day I will have to leave to the psychiatrists of our era. That is way beyond my pay grade, and I'm sure actually bewilders many of them. At times the nuclear family is just plain nuked, although many "How to" books have been written, a few of which you, the reader, may have read.

An incident that stays in my mind to bolster my dad-ability concerns my daughter. She was a few years into her teens with beautiful long red hair, a gorgeous face, and among the smartest in her class.

One evening the doorbell to our garden apartment rang. The kids were watching television, so I went to the door, asked who it was, and received no answer. I turned the doorknob, and, as I did so, I heard the thundering clash of glass right outside the door. I opened the door gingerly and saw the shattered remains of a milk bottle, and the ungodly smell of urine splashed throughout the hallway.

Some one had half filled a milk bottle with urine and placed it on top of the outside doorknob, so that anyone opening the door by turning the knob would cause the bottle to fall and leave the ensuing mess. I knew it wasn't the landlord, as we always paid our bills.

My kids came running to the door to see what was happening. I was in shock. We all stood there looking at a sight, or should I say mess, that was unbelievable. Finally my daughter broke the silence.

"I know who did that," she said. Then she named the culprit, a young boy who was always trying to get her attention in school.

"How do you know?" I asked.

"I know. He's always bothering me in school. This is just like him. He was bothering me today."

"What's his telephone number?"

"I don't know."

We looked up his last name in the telephone book, and, fortunately, there was only one person listed under that name.

I took a chance, called and asked, "Is this...?" (I don't want to advertise his misdeeds at this point in life.)

"Yes," came a hesitant reply.

"Well this is Mr. O'Farrell, Anne Marie's father," I roared. I was going for a home run. Silence on the other end of the phone. Loooong silence. This was every indication that I had the right culprit. As the silence continued, no reply came from the other end of the phone.

I gambled. "We know what you did, and I want you to be in front of my house in five minutes." He only lived one block away. "And if you're not here, I'll come over to your house and kick the shit out of you." This was the first time my children heard me use the word "shit", and they were more frightened than the young teen-ager.

Now I had a problem. I would go out front and do what? I couldn't punch a teen-age kid. If I punched anybody I would be breaking the law, because the fists of fighters are considered lethal weapons, and I had been a professional fighter. What about retired fighters, I pondered. I wasn't sure, and I really didn't want to belt anybody.

But the kid solved my problem. He came walking down the street with his six foot two brother. That really solved the belting problem. I'm practical if not bright. Still, what do I do?

The only answer seemed to be rebuking the lad with my "teacher's voice." This is a harsh, vociferous tone I used when I was scolding a student in the school in which I taught. My words have an inordinate tone meant to convey, "I'll kill you if you do it again." Of course, it's phony, something I picked up in my acting ventures, ventures I won't go into in this book.

It worked as the boy stood there, his head bowed low in an, "I won't do it again," stance. And when I was through with my rant he said to me almost on cue, "I'm sorry. I won't do anything like this again." Then he finished what was really his prime fear. "You won't tell my father, will you?"

The picture was now complete. His father had the six foot two brother and him in vivid fear of their lives. Poppa knew nothing of what had happened, and they must have told him they were going out for a walk as they trolled over to my house.

His father was the solution to my problem, as I'm sure Poppa belted them around a good bit, judging from the pleading of his tone.

"I'll think about it," I said knowing I wouldn't. My anger turned to relief as I walked back into my apartment and told my kids, "I really took care of him."

They were thrilled with their own stand-up Dad, and never learned what happened outside the apartment house in that early evening. I was a hero again, but this time under false pretenses. That night I was a "good Dad" in their eyes.

◆　◆　◆

I realize this is a prologue to Little Jim's and Anne Marie's tales so let me turn to my son.

He certainly enjoyed going to the gymnasium and watching boxers train. He recently reminded me of a circus I took him to at which Emile Griffith, then Welterweight Champion, was parading around a little white poodle, all the while being dressed as a clown.

Jim remembers nothing of his being hit by a truck when he was almost six years old. The mind has a happy facility of shutting out things it prefers not to remember. Not always, but thank God in this instance, although it certainly was the worst day of my life.

I have finished this prologue before Jim begins his book, "My Dad or Why Did God Choose Me?" He has a great sense of humor and I'm sure he will kid around about me. I have my fingers crossed. If he tells the truth about me, I'm dead. Go get 'em Tiger. I'll start you off.

Dad's Tale

Includes:

- Rocky Marciano
- Mario Cuomo
- Joe Louis
- Jack Newfield
- "Maria" of *Sesame Street*
- George Foreman
- Wendy Barrie
- Emile Griffith
- Gil Clancy, T.V. Commentator
- David Lerner

How do you like that kid? My kid, I mean. *My Dad* or *Why Did God Choose Me?*

What? He's *unhappy* that God chose him to be my son? Or he's *happy* that God chose him? He can play that title anyway he wants. Poor little Jim, he got stuck with me as his father.

Or, how lucky he was to be born with yours truly as his dad? I'll be damned if I know. Anyhow, the fact that he allowed me to open his book telling my side of the story permits me to live with the assumption that he's happy that I'm his dad.

Sure he is.

Seriously, (which is hard to be with a rascal like my son) if you believe everything he tells you about me, your middle name must be "Gullibility." Or doth I protest too quickly?

I was able to talk him into including my daughter, Anne Marie, and her version of life in the O'Farrell family in his book.

No way it can come out as a Eugene O'Neil saga. I hope my daughter writes a balanced view of *Life with Father.* Hear that A.M.? I almost never called my little redhead "Anne Marie." Always A.M. I've had a habit of making up nicknames for people and making them live with the nickname.

For example, I always called my father "Jocko," which, of course, was not his true name. Even when someone told me "Jocko" was the nickname for an organ grinder's monkey. I meant no disrespect, but still I always told my two kids we were going over to "Jocko's" house this weekend.

To cliché a cliché—old habits die hard.

♦   ♦   ♦

Speaking of my own father there are pictures all around the house of my father and his friend showing me how to hold my hands up in a boxer's position. I was only four years old, but there I was with my left hand out front, preparing to left jab, and my right hand in a position to throw a right cross which was intended to be the knockout punch. And I can't count the number of times I'd find myself in a YMCA being taught how to punch the heavy sand bag.

I was too small to reach the "speed" bag, which is the one you see in the movies going rat-a-tat-tat. That was way over my head when I was four.

By the time I was twelve Pop entered me in a P.A.L. tournament. I was ninety pounds, and the tournament had a ninety-pound division. I fought my way to the finals, (remember, they had been training me since I was four) which were held in the open air in summertime at Sheridan Square, Greenwich Village, where I fought the best fight of my life and was crowned Champion of the ninety pound fighters. I also received the best write-up from a local paper, a write-up that I trot out to show friends (and enemies) whenever my ego needs up-lifting.

I never mention that my opponent didn't know a thing about boxing, and was petrified by the five thousand spectators who were cheering as if it were World War II. Poor kid looked like he just wanted to go home to Momma, and who the Hell put him in this tournament, let alone fighting an opponent who had been training eight years, from four to twelve. Me.

Not only was I training in the gym, but also I was being physically built up in all sorts of manners. I was sent to a farm upstate when I was ten years old to fill out my slender physique. When I tell the story I label it, "How I spent a summer on a farm one day."

The farmer picked me up at the train station early in the evening in which I arrived, fed me, and showed me to my bedroom. As I was unpacking he left the room saying, "See you in the morning." It was seven P.M. "What about the evening," I thought to myself. Was he a religious man who wanted me to pray for two hours?

I found out fifteen minutes later as he knocked on my door and entered.

"You not in bed yet?"

"Not yet sir," I answered.

"Better hurry," was the reply.

Hurry what? It's quarter after seven in the evening and this man is hustling me off to bed! The curse words I had just learned in my neighborhood in the Bronx rattled around in my head, but I figured I had better say Our Fathers and Hail Mary's, as I was in foreign territory and the Good Lord had better get Himself by my side. But I soon fell off to sleep.

However, the pesky farmer was back again, shaking me and saying things like "It's time to get up."

"How come?" I queried. As I spoke, I looked out the window. It was black outside. Pitch black!

"It's three o'clock, Boy," he replied. "Breakfast is ready and you got to eat and get out pitching."

Was he kidding? It's three o'clock in the morning and he's waking me up to do some pitching. I played second base on my neighborhood team and I couldn't pitch. Especially in the middle of the night.

I got up, got dressed, and went downstairs to a bowl of oatmeal. The farmer left the table, got his truck and drove up to the house yelling, "Let's Go."

I gulped my last spoonful and staggered to his truck wondering how I could pitch at four o'clock, when even the morning had not yet awakened. And where is the rest of the team? And where are we going to play baseball?

He drove quickly to a large barn, said, "Get out," which I did, because I realized I was dealing with a man bereft of his senses. He handed me what I later learned was a pitchfork, told me to get up there on the hay loft, and told me to pitch the hay on the open back of the truck, while he sauntered off to do what he called "chores."

This was murder. My arms ached after half an hour and I realized neither Mary nor Jesus was going to answer my prayers. Or help me pitch!

He said, "That's enough for now," as he saw the hay in the back of the truck filled with my sweat. I realized that insanity was this man's first name as he said, "now we'll do some real chores."

Now do you believe they started me at age 4?

PARK WEST BOYS' CLUBS SUCCESSFUL

The following members of the Park West Neighborhood Association, under the direction of Mr. Sargis, competed in a monster boxing show given under the auspices of the Police Athletic League on May 24, at Sheridan Square Manhattan.

Bill Davidson who is the champion in the 70 lb. class won his bout by a close margin. Bill outboxed his opponent, at close quarters and they were pounding away at each other with Billy having the upper hand.

Jackie Scott, who fought in the 105 lb. class, was clowning with his opponent until he realized he was on his way to defeat. Jackie fought like a mad man and matched his opponent two punches for one in the late stage of the fight.

William Aguiar, who fought in the 115 lb. class, had to come from behind to win his bout. William had to slug his opponent very badly in the lastround to win.

The best bout was fought by Jimmy O'Farrell in the 90 lb. class. Jim kept left jabbing and upper cutting his opponent with both hands, from the first to the third round. The spectators were praising Jim for the magnificent way in which he handled his opponent.

So help me I do not know this writer.
I couldn't have paid for this last paragraph.

I have to skip the "real chores" part, which we did until lunch (ten-thirty), so I can tell you what my scheming mind worked out.

Came lunch, and, as we sat at the table, I managed to choke down some crocodile tears until the farmer's wife finally asked me "What's the matter, Son."

"It's my mother," was my answer. "She started running a fever when I left home, and when I kissed her goodbye I could feel the heat in her cheeks." Then I began to cry for real, except I was crying for me being in this God-forsaken place.

Both the farmer and his wife became upset and the wife came to me, put her arms around my shaking and heaving shoulders and asked "Would you like to call home and find out how she is?"

"Could I, please?"

"Of course, Son," as she pointed to the telephone. I dashed and dialed and the phone rang and rang.

"What," I screamed into a ringing telephone. "Pop, I have to get to that hospital right away. I'm coming home right now," and hung up to a still ringing telephone.

"What is it?" the wife queried. Her face was wrinkled and worried.

"Sickle cell pneumonia," I screamed. "She's in a hospital. They don't know if she'll make it." I was beside myself.

"There is a one o'clock train to New York. I'll get you on it," the farmer blurted as he rushed upstairs to help me pack.

"Oh thank you, Sir," I murmured in a manner that would have made Charles Dickens proud.

We rushed, caught the train, and on the way home I worried what my new friends would think when they received a phone bill later that month with no charge to New York. A sympathetic telephone operator? Could be!

And that's how I spent a summer on a farm one day! Make it half a day. We city boys aren't cut out for the hard work the farmers endure, God bless them. They are more rugged than we will ever be, which is how we win wars. The farmers do it! They nurture us with what they grow and harvest, and those who aren't fighting are taking care of those who do. Once again, God bless them and forgive me for my youthful indiscretion.

Jim, I don't think I ever told you about that summer story. Now, whenever the topic comes up, you can chime in and say, "Oh, my father worked on a farm when he was young. Farms help you to build up your muscles. That's what gave him his knockout punch!" Just don't mention it was half a day.

◆　◆　◆

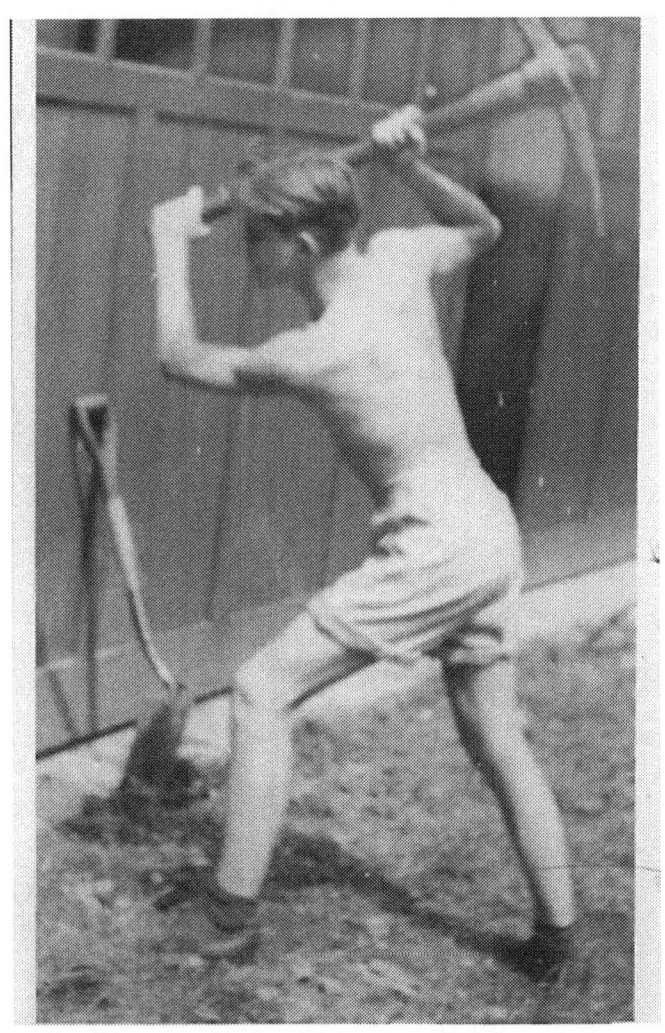

Farming isn't just pitching hay! Pick and shovel are also body builders. Particularly since you drop from exhaustion. But who's complaining?

I'll move on to a world I knew better, The Bronx.

I barely got by in school. Every day at 3:00 o'clock I left school to train at a CYO gym downtown, costing me three hours, getting home just in time for dinner, and I was competing against all my friends who were Jewish. Those guys were voracious students and knew every subject backwards and forwards.

My parents didn't have any money to send me to a Catholic school, and my classmates were all future Kissingers and Einsteins. Did they have brains, Wow!

When I was seventeen I scraped under the fence of graduation from high school, Taft High School. Don't ask me how.

Edye Gorme and Steve Lawrence graduated from Taft a few years after me and eventually married and became first class singers throughout the country.

World War II was raging and I figured I could lick the Japs and Nazis with one hand tied behind my back, so I enlisted in the Navy.

Sampson Naval Base was my destination and I was assigned to a barracks with about one hundred and twenty men. I heard they had "smokers," fights, every Friday, so I sought out the gym.

One day the chief saw me working out and he questioned my past pugilistic experience. When I told him, he became tremendously excited, and with a flushed face he whispered into my ear, "Us chiefs bet on the Friday fights, and my money is going to be on you."

Spotting an opening I answered back, "Just a minute Chief, these conditions here are bad for a trained fighter. When I was ninety pounds I won a CYO championship in a tournament where the finals were held outdoors in Sheridan Square before five thousand people. I got great write-ups in a local Greenwich Village paper. I'm one hundred twenty six pounds and I have to get more sleep and eat even better now."

"You'll eat steak," he yelled, "plenty of steak, all you want, don't worry, don't worry, I'll arrange it!"

He could see a potential meal ticket slipping away and he was trying to nail me down. The dollar bills he could make with me were not about to get away from him. I saw his desperation and pushed.

"But getting up at seven in the morning leaves me tired all day. I just can't do it."

"Who says you have to get up at seven? I'll leave orders you are to be allowed to sleep until eight. How's that?" I was tempted to ask for a percentage of what he won, but thought better of it.

At the same time he began having second thoughts about my veracity.

"How many fights have you had?" he questioned.

Now I was starting to get teed off.

"Listen, when I was fifteen I fought the one hundred and eighteen pound champ at the coast guard station at Hoffman Island for the CYO."

"Wait a minute," he said. "You have to be twenty one to get into the Coast Guard."

"Sure," I replied, but I was the only one hundred twenty pound fighter we had, so my trainer volunteered me. I didn't like fighting a twenty one year old Coast Guard Champion, but I did.

"How did you do?'

"They called it a draw, but I kicked the crap out of him."

He thought for a moment. "Of course they called it a draw," he realized. "He was the 'Hometown Boy'. That makes sense."

"Same thing happened to me in Stamford, Conn. I fought the 'Hometown Boy', beat the Hell out of him and they called it a draw too. His manager apologized to me after the fight."

The chief could see by the fury in my face as I relived the two bad decisions, I was being truthful. Just thinking about being robbed twice made me want to kill.

"You're my man O'Farrell. How will you do here?"

"I can lick every man at Sampson." That was my first exaggeration, and what a whopper.

"Steak and eight o'clock," he yelled as he ran to make arrangements. "You better come through."

Right then I was tempted to ask for a cut of his winnings, but greed wasn't a part of my nature. But…never mind. Steak and an extra hour of sleep would have to suffice.

I did win every Friday night and when the big tournament came up I won the championship. However, and I have to admit this, most of my opponents never had a glove on in their lives. They were in it for the fun. I was in it for the steak and sleep. Not one opponent knew how to fight. It was a breeze. I never tell that to anybody. Just that I won the championship. Please don't tell anybody!

Quartermaster school was my next assignment. Twelve weeks of learning how to "shoot the stars" with a sextant on the bridge which plotted the ship's course, and learning the Morse Code by lights and radio. Many ships did not have signalmen aboard, so the Q.M. had to learn their jobs.

After we finished Q.M. school we were given a slip of paper questioning what type of ship we wanted to be assigned to, e.g. battleship, destroyer, etc.

I gave it much thought and came to the conclusion that the only ships that had females aboard were Red Cross ships, dozens and dozens of beautiful nurses. Consequently, I listed the three choices of ships I preferred. Red Cross, Red Cross, Red Cross. They asked for my three preferences and that's what I gave them.

That's not what they gave me. I can just picture the officer in charge of handing out assignments saying to himself, "That cowardly S.O.B. O'Farrell wants a ship that the enemy is not permitted to shoot at. I'll give him something that will turn his yellow streak into diarrhea. A minesweeper!!!"

Obviously he didn't understand. Damn him, a minesweeper it was. No nurses, just a bunch of hot headed guys on a ship that swept mines for the invasion of Normandy and the coming invasion of Japan. Sometimes I am very misunderstood.

◆　◆　◆

While at Q.M. school I went AWOL, absent without leave. We were given every other weekend off to go into Buffalo, Friday night to Sunday night. One weekend I figured I'd take the alternate weekend, the one I was supposed to remain on base, and sneaked into town when it was not my turn to have leave until next Friday.

Wouldn't you know? They had bed check that Friday night and O'Farrell was missing. That's AWOL unless I'm dead somewhere.

Monday morning I was told to report to a particular officer's office, first thing before breakfast. Some other idiot had to go also, and we went together. I figured brig time, maybe a month.

I knocked at the officer's door and a gruff take-charge voice shouted, "Come in." My compatriot shuffled in alongside me, and we found ourselves facing a thirty-odd year old husky man standing in his shorts, and nothing else. His breath reeked of gin and his red eyes betrayed him.

He wasn't embarrassed at his undress, so I figured why should I be perturbed. Hell, he was an officer, no matter how he was undressed, and shorts or no shorts he held my future in his hands.

I saluted smartly and sharply and called out, "O'Farrell Sir." My salute was as brilliant as I could make it, and he finally saluted me back. He was more flummoxed than I was scared. I was trying to look like the bravest most honorable sailor in the U.S. Navy. My morose companion, who was sure he was going to do time in a Navy jail, just kept looking at the floor, no salute, no confidence, just complete resignation.

The officer looked at us both and said, "O'Farrell you look like a good man. They must have made a mistake. You're dismissed. You can go back to your company." What a sharp salute could accomplish!

"Aye aye Sir," was my reply as I walked with great confidence to the door and fled like a deer before he could change his mind. I saluted again just to make sure.

I was the salutingest sailor in the United States Navy. I told my buddies, whenever you're in trouble just salute. It massages the officers' egos. They love to be saluted.

◆ ◆ ◆

Case in example. I went to a theatre in Buffalo with a buddy (on a legitimate leave). We were standing outside the movie house ready to enter when I saw seven young officers coming my way.

Quickly I said to my cohort, "I'll stand here right outside the theatre and you stand ten feet to my right. When they reach me, I'll salute, and all seven will have to salute me back. Then when they reach you a few feet away from me, you salute, and all seven will have to salute you back. That way, seven officers will have to salute twice, you and me."

As they were passing by me I saluted, and all seven instead of continuing on their way past the theatre, turned and walked over to me.

"Oh my God," I thought. "They know me and they'll march me off to the brig."

Instead, each one dug into his pocket, came out with a one-dollar bill, and handed it to me. Seven dollars! My buddy, suspecting something foul was happening, came running over shouting, "What's the matter?"

The seventh officer explained. "It's O.K. We just graduated from the Academy and we have to give one dollar to the first man who saluted us. You were the first," he grinned, and trotted off to join his six buddy officers who were now past the theatre.

My depressed partner heard the explanation and bitched, "Damn you, you put me a little further past you and so you got the seven bucks."

I bawled him out. "If you had stayed in your position, they would have had to salute you also."

"Yeah, but I wouldn't have gotten the seven bucks."

"I'll split it with you, Dummy," I retorted. "If you had followed my orders at least all seven of them would have had to salute again. No more money, but more inconvenience for them."

"Aye, aye Sir," he grinned as he saluted me.

"I'm not an officer, but I'll drag you into the movie with their money. I'm not cheap, cause I'm not an officer yet. Did you see the looks on their faces? Like now they're broke. One dollar each, huh. But you didn't keep your position and cause them to salute again."

"I said, aye, aye Sir, didn't I?" his grinning face exploded. He then saluted me laughing like Hell.

"Here's a buck," I howled. Did we enjoy that movie!

In the meantime the chief I had before quartermaster school was still cleaning up from my Q.M. smoker bouts, but the Q.M. school chief wasn't a betting man, so I was back to rising from my cot at seven A.M. and eating what everyone else ate.

After Q.M. school I boarded the blasted ship, but as we headed for the invasion of Japan I was seasick, up-chucking almost every day. Why didn't I get that big Red Cross ship instead of a tiny minesweeper with only twenty-four men aboard? Bad luck, or divine intervention? Sometimes God doesn't pay attention, or maybe He thought I shouldn't be chasing nurses and this was His punishment.

We dropped the bomb at Hiroshima and I was spared a sure fire fatality in this planned second invasion. Minesweepers in invasions are the first ones in, though you wouldn't know it watching the movies. They almost never show "Sweeps," just the soldiers landing. The Army and Marines would be blown out of the water if we minesweepers didn't sweep all the enemy mines awaiting invasions. Our ship turned around during the surrender, and after much deliberation this lucky sailor was discharged. Amen!

I realize the havoc reeked upon Japan that week in August. We celebrate the dropping of the bomb, and they celebrate, or rather mourn, their great losses. In all honesty, I doubt if I would be alive and writing this if we had invaded.

War is disaster for everybody, going back to the cavemen tribes thousands of years ago. It has led me to believe this is the planet of rejects. Conflicts seem to be as constant as breathing. My son-in-law, Ricky Stack, is a "New Age" devotee, and we constantly debate the character of man. He is convinced, through the spirit guide "Seth," Jane Roberts's voice from beyond, that we are entering a period where all will be well with mankind. I believe in Thomas Aquinas's version that man is more *inclined* toward evil, rather than good. The operative word is *"inclined."*

After my Navy days were over I thought it was wise to join a club. A very distinguished club, populated by ex-servicemen. It was called the 52/20 club.

It went like this. As a discharged serviceman you were allowed to go to a particular office near your home, in my case on the Grand Concourse in the Bronx, and fill out an application. The application asked all the pertinent questions, i.e.

name, rank, etc. One of the questions asked was what type of work was appropriate for you to engage in, now that you were discharged.

If you did not have employment, you had to go to the above-mentioned office where a kindly gentleman questioned you, and, if you did not have employment, this helpful employee would find a job that fit your particular field of endeavor.

You were to report to him each week seeking his help. In the meantime, as you were waiting for employment in your special field, the service, i.e. Navy in my case, would send you a check for twenty dollars weekly. However, this lasted only fifty-two weeks, one year. When the year was up, the twenty-dollar check was just a memory if they had not been able to send you out to apply for work successfully, or if you found a job on your own.

The first week I entered the office, I filled out the application and presented it to the genial gentleman, who at that moment was sorting out other applications. This was a very popular club, with many wishing to join.

I sat opposite him as he shuffled through those who wanted to enroll. Then he came to mine. He smiled appreciatively, as his job depended on how may applicants he could help.

"O.K., Jim," he said, "let's see how we can help you."

I was pleased he called me by my first name, as this appeared to be a promising relationship between us. A long relationship. A very, very long relationship. Perhaps he would invite me to dinner at his house once we got to know each other.

He glanced at my application murmuring to himself, "Let's see name, address, Navy, type employ…"

He never did finish that last word. When he got to "ment," he screamed "*FIGHTER?*"

"Yes sir," I answered with dispatch. "I hope this hasn't upset you. My mother feels the same as you. She had wanted me to retire for many years before I enlisted in the Navy, but I felt my obligation to Uncle Sam should be fulfilled before I selfishly fought for myself. I'm not a selfish individual."

I almost saluted, considering my past experience with a snappy salute, but I contained myself.

"I've gotten all kinds of jobs for you guys," he sputtered as his face was turning beet red. "But I never came across nothing like this."

His use of a double negative indicated he never had been an Officer, or if so a lousy one.

"It's quite easy," I offered. "You call up Madison Square Garden and tell them you have a fighter who wants to fight in MSG."

"But I'm not a manager," he exploded.

"Well, Sir, I know you'll do your best."

I rose from the chair more than anxious to leave.

"What the Hell do I do," he called at me as I approached the exit door.

"You do what they tell us in the Navy. The best you can."

"Damn you, you'll get your checks. I'm not going to call up Madison Square Garden. They'll think I'm crazy. Damn you, damn you, damn you."

Now I know he had never been an Officer. They don't curse, particularly not in triplicate. I was certain I would not be invited to his house for dinner; nevertheless, I had a relaxing year.

I was anxious to get to college when my year of checks ran out, but so was every other G.I.; therefore colleges were filled to the brim. Uncle Sam was footing college bills, depending on how long one had served.

I was back in the gym, even though my 52/20 sponsor was of no help. I mentioned to my trainer, Pete Mello, who handled the CYO training edifice at 17th Street in Manhattan that I'd like to get into a college.

While I was waiting for any word, Rocky Marciano showed up from Brockton, Mass. He was one of the worst heavyweights I had ever seen in a gymnasium. Rock had the good luck to have the best trainer in the history of boxing, "Little" Charlie Goldman. Charlie was only 5 foot tall, and 120 pounds, but he had fought 140 fights, consequently, he knew all there was to know about boxing and training fighters.

Rocky was just a wild swinging fighter with a tremendous punch, but no knowledge of form or short punches. Charlie didn't let Rock spar with anyone for three weeks, preferring to teach him to shorten his punches.

Marciano improved 300 percent under Goldman's tutelage and when "the Rock" finally did spar with a sparring mate, he knocked him cold in the 2nd round.

I remember the first day he and I worked out together and left the gym together. Rocky was living in a boarding house on 92nd Street and the subway was on 14th Street and 7th Avenue. We were between 9th & 10th Avenues, and as we left, Marciano filled me in on the few fights he had fought in Brockton.

As we reached 7th Avenue I took the heavyweight by the arm to steer him to the subway at 14th Street. He said, "No, Jim, I'm going to walk to 92nd Street. That's where I'm rooming while I'm in New York. They call it Ma Brown's boarding house."

"Rock, that's more than three miles," I gasped. "Did you do road work this morning?"

"Sure, but things like that are going to make me a champ." That's when I started to become a believer. Afterwards he went on to become an all-time great, along with Louis and Ali.

Often in later years he would call me at home to have dinner at Mama Leone's or lunch at Danny's Hideaway. He was so soft spoken, and so unassuming, it was hard to believe he could kill you with one punch.

One night at Mama Leone's restaurant, this elderly thin man came over. I should say stumbled over, confronted Rocky and slurred, "I can lick you."

Marciano used an old Jimmy Durante joke. Durante, in his unique style, told the story about the little mouse and the towering elephant, wherein the elephant looked down at the mouse and said, "Look at you, you're a tiny insignificant nothing, and I'm a big, strong, powerful creature." To which the mouse answered, "But I've been sick."

Rocky without missing a beat, looked at his elder, and with a straight face and an innocent look said, "But I've been sick."

Everyone nearby cracked up as the waiters helped the aged one back to his table.

One of the advantages of eating in good restaurants with the champ was it was always "on the arm," literally meaning no check. The restaurateurs loved having him in their establishments. I miss Rocky to this day. I could fill another book with Tales of Rocky, but that will have to wait.

Meanwhile, back at the ranch, which means the gym, my trainer had news for me.

"Jack LaValle told us you should see him about college."

"Who is Jack LaValle?"

"You don't know? He's the chief football scout for Notre Dame, and the football Giants. He's also head of the CYO in New York. He saw you knockout that guy at the Glenn Island Casino Park and he's always calling to find out when you're going to fight again."

"There were Fifteen thousand people that night," I said, "and he was one of them?"

"You bet," Pete answered. "Call the Powerhouse and make an appointment to see him."

"What's the Powerhouse," I asked.

"The Catholic Diocese on Fiftieth Street," came the reply.

I did, and I met Mr. LaValle who said, "Call me Jack."

I was soon registered to enter Fordham University for the September session, and I was to report to 302 Broadway, which was the School of Education. I always wanted to teach and this was beyond my dreams.

However, before October was over, I realized I could not go to school, go to the gym, and study late into the night. Something had to give.

It was boxing. The grueling days clouded my mind and I decided if I wanted to get out of Fordham in less than 4 years, something had to go. I got out in 2 years and 9 months, and felt like I was an old man. Summer school, extra credits, veterans were allowed to take the whole magilla. I had already won 3 championships and, as they say, I had to move forward.

I know I was remembered for many years at the University for my entrepreneurship. Not my scholarship, my entrepreneurship.

When I was in my senior year all the talk was about buying school rings. The price was high and some students couldn't afford to buy one. Yet they really wanted a ring, they were so beautiful.

The address, 302 Broadway, was right next to the jewelry district. I borrowed a ring from a friend of mine who had graduated the year before me, and went into the heart of the district.

I picked out a jewelry manufacturer and went up to the loft with the ring.

"I want to see the boss," I accosted a young employee.

"I am the boss and you're too young to see anybody," he smiled.

"And you're too young to be the boss," I laughed.

"No," he grinned, "truthfully I am the boss, even though I look as young as you."

"Good, now we can get down to business. See this ring?" I showed him the Fordham ring. "Can you duplicate it?"

He looked it over carefully.

"Of course. It's easy."

"How much?" I asked. He quoted me a price ten dollars below what the University was asking.

"Not good enough." I took the ring back and started for the door.

"Wait a minute. How many rings will you order?"

"Around twenty," my scared bones were tingling in my body. How could I know if I could sell twenty, and how could I know if they would come out exact replicas.

"And throw one in for me for free," the words rang through the air and my mouth was open, so I must have been the one to say it. He then lowered the price another ten dollars when he heard an order for twenty rings.

"Deal," I said. "When can you have them for me?"

"Three days."

It was all consummated, the rings were ready, I gave him a check and told him not to cash it for a week, and somehow he trusted me.

Three days later I picked up 21 rings, scooted over to school and the rings disappeared like magic to twenty students who were paying ten dollars less than the school was charging. Exact duplicates and everybody was happy and I was mucho richer.

Two weeks later the ramifications began.

I was sitting in English class when a student opened the door from outside, handed the professor a note and stood next to his desk waiting.

"Mr. O'Farrell, you'll have to go with this student to see Miss Scanlon."

Miss Scanlon was a beautiful dean who could lick Rocky Marciano. Everybody was terrified of her, yours truly included.

I marched, and I do mean marched, with this student to Miss Scanlon's door. The student left. I would have laid ten to one there was a guillotine inside.

I knocked on the door.

"Come in," a shrill voice.

I said to myself "I've fought the best fighters in the world, why should I be afraid of a little old lady."

She wasn't old, she wasn't little, but she was blonde and beautiful, with the reputation of a Viking.

"Sit down" she ordered. Her face was stone.

"I love your hair style," I conned. "Before we discuss anything may I be so bold as to ask you where you have your hair done."

Mount Rushmore was crumbling. She gave me a name and address and I whipped out a pen and a notebook and scribbled.

"I have to tell my sister," I continued. The con worked, but just momentarily.

"Mr. O'Farrell, are you the one who has been selling our rings?"

"Yes, ma'am," my innocent face was working overtime.

"Do you think that's ethical?"

Now my fighter's adrenalin took over and little Mr. Innocent disappeared as I said firmly and with roaring fervor. Isn't this a capitalist country or did I fight a war for nothing?"

No one, not even God, spoke to Miss Scanlon like this.

"You can go back to your class now," she stammered.

I got up, walked to the door, opened it, sneaked a look back and saw her fixing her hair.

I graduated with honor; the honor of beating Miss Scanlon, a very singular honor in as much as I have no sister. I'm an only child, but one with a Degree. You know, I think Miss Scanlon would have beaten Rocky Marciano.

◆　◆　◆

When I think of the Rock it always brings me back to the very last fight of my life (in the ring).

It was, in its own ways, Marciano redux. You know how I described the wild swinging newcomer from Brockton? Wild swinging, no form, just sheer brutality. Well, in the last fight of my career I came up against the very same style.

The bell rang opening the first round and this tiger came rushing across the ring at me swinging punches from left field, right field, and center field. When I say, "swinging" I don't mean "throwing" punches, I mean a snowstorm of rights and lefts seemed to be coming from the sky. The clouds were opening up and it was literally raining punches aimed to kill.

This can be very disturbing, actually causing you to tuck in your head, primarily your chin, and fall inside the fusillade that is raining all around you, but if you're smart you tuck in close to the bomber who is trying to kill you, tie up his arms in a clinch, and think fast. I hated to fight a pugilist who knows no form, just "kill, kill, kill."

I thought fast that night. Before the referee could break us from the clinch I started whispering in my opponent's ear.

"Are you crazy? You'll never last till the end. Pace yourself, and save something for the rest of our fight. Pace yourself."

The ref broke the clinch, and my opponent stepped back and stood there like a statue. I think he thought it was God talking to him and telling him in effect "Go easy."

He stopped throwing his flying missiles and struck a pose, like a normal fighter usually does.

I waited one second and he didn't move, just posed, because someone whispered in his ear to pace himself, and perhaps that's what he should do considering he had just gotten some good advice, disregarding the source of that advice. His opponent, ME!

I didn't wait for the second moment to pass, lest he realize maybe it was not his style to hesitate, and then go back to being a wild energizer bunny. Before the next second passed I stepped in hit him with a left-right combo, right on his chin.

Boom, he fell face forward on the canvas, and before the referee told me to go to a neutral corner, I bent over and whispered in his ear, "that's how you're suppose to punch, straight, not round house." I was hoping to ease his pain!

The count of ten was unnecessary as they carried him back to his corner. I figured I'd better get upstairs and take a shower, get dressed and get the Hell out of there.

While I'm taking the shower, supremely satisfied with myself, the door to the shower room opened.

There, still in his trunks, but with his gloves off, stood my conned ex-opponent.

"Oh, oh" I thought to myself. "There's no one in this shower room but the two of us and those missiles are going to start zooming at me. Couldn't he be a good sport and let bygones be bygones?"

He approached me as I was still under the shower; stood still for a moment and put out his right hand. "You're the fairest fighter I ever fought," he said.

I shook his right hand even though my hand was soaking wet and replied, "I was trying to help you, but as time goes by you'll learn." He thanked me profusely. This was surrealistic. I hoped he wouldn't ask for my autograph!

◆ ◆ ◆

Now I could get on with teaching. The idea of imparting knowledge to others was always a joy. I loved to see people learn and progress, particularly youngsters.

When an advertisement for teachers at a Junior High School in Harlem appeared in a newspaper I was elated. The morning after the ad appeared I drove to the school and asked to see the principal. I was shown into the office of a frail woman seated at a desk overlooking the schoolyard. (No, I didn't salute.)

"I'm Mr. O'Farrell, and I'm answering the ad for a teacher."

She motioned to a chair opposite her desk, and I quickly seated myself spewing out my credentials, e.g., "I have a degree in secondary education and I graduated Fordham."

"You didn't graduate Fordham, they graduated you. And you're an English major?" she snapped.

I realized I had been chastised properly and sat meekly waiting for the next round. And so help me she was only ninety pounds.

She studied me as though I were an anthological freak. Then she looked out the window and watched the children playing in the schoolyard. Minutes passed. I had a bad feeling. Then she looked at me, back to the kids playing outside. Her head started moving from left to right. I was feeling worse.

"See those kids playing out there?" she asked.

I nodded and wondered what her next sentence would be.

Slowly she said, "They'll eat you alive."

I had no idea what she was talking about.

'They're fourteen and fifteen years old," she started. "They can be very rough to handle. I'm afraid I can't hire you, but thanks for coming." She went back to the papers on her desk. I was duly dismissed.

I rose from the chair and headed for the door. I took one last look out the window at the kids playing tag or whatever. I had spent the better part of my life fighting the best fighters in the world and I wouldn't be able to handle these teenage babies? Wonders really never cease.

I'm sure she hired a twenty-one year old girl with a shrill voice, a very shrill voice. I doubt if the new teacher she would hire had a good right cross!

It took days for me to come out of my daze. I did, finally, and answered another ad for a Junior High School in the Bronx. Turned out it was a girl's school, and the principal, 80 year old Alice McCormack, told me in our interview she would hire me, even though I would be the first male teacher in the history of the school.

This had to be a breeze until I found out the girls screamed at the garbage collector, age sixty-five, the mailman, age fifty-three, like the Rolling Stones had entered their haven.

I had to have my phone number changed three times in the first month, till I remembered you could have an unlisted number. Even then the phone calls didn't stop completely.

After one year I realized the energy could be harnessed. I noticed there was great talent in the school, talent of an artistic nature. I talked the principal into allowing me to start a drama class. The idea caught on and this led to a music class wherein the girls learned singing, playing instruments, and, finally, a dance class. All of this in addition to regular studies.

I had heard of the Bronx House Music School, a school not five miles away, which gave lessons to especially talented students at a reasonable price.

Andrew McKinley, a T.V. star, ran the school. I made a trip to see Mr. McKinley, begging for a special price for our students, the ones we selected, to go there.

Andrew insisted he come to our school to try-out the ones we selected. If he agreed they had talent he would give us a discount for lessons at his special school. He came each year, auditioned the singers and dancers, and we got our special price.

◆   ◆   ◆

Now the drama. The famous High School of Performing Arts was next in my sights. I trained my drama students to audition for this great high school, which turned out many, many actors and actresses who went on to the Broadway stage, T.V. and movies. Twenty-one out of twenty-four were selected.

Sesame Street almost missed out on their most famous star "Maria."

Maria's real name is Sonia Manzano. She was in my acting class because I persuaded her to give it a try. She agreed rather reluctantly, not particularly thrilled with acting. She was good enough to audition for Performing Acts High School, but she didn't want to go there. Also, her parents wanted her to go to a different high school.

I made a deal with her.

"If I can talk your parents into letting you go to the Performing Arts will you audition for the school?"

She made a face and said "O.K."

"I'll tell you what. Your mother and father finish eating by eight o'clock, right? Tomorrow night at eight thirty I'll be at your apartment. Tell them I'm coming to talk with them. I'll explain everything and we'll see what they'll say."

She shrugged a quizzical ascent and looked at me like I was from another planet.

At eight thirty the next night the greatest pitchman in America rang Sonia's doorbell. I made The Music Man look like a stutterer.

Net result. Your children grew up with "Maria" of Sesame Street A.K.A. Sonia Manzano of the South Bronx. If I had any brains I would have become her agent. There is more than one dumb Irishman around!

One of our dancers, Sally Neal, toured the world with two other girls, another Sandra Gallardo, appeared with Charles Bronson in Death Wish II.

I had been able to raise over twenty thousand dollars in ten years by producing plays such as The Music Man, Twelve Angry Men, The Mikado, et al, charging admission at our Junior High School, enabling our talent to enrich their innate abilities at the Bronx House Music School, and progress from there. Can't leave Performing Arts out, although there was no charge as this was a public school.

◆   ◆   ◆

I was on a roll, but there was little money coming in to my household. One of my student's mother had just graduated from beauty school. The parent's name was Marie Castro. I had met her at a teacher-parent conference. She was an attractive woman, hair, of course, well styled.

In as much as I was well known in the neighborhood because of the shows I was putting on, I thought I'd roll the dice. I met with Mrs. Castro and suggested we open a beauty parlor. I, obviously, knew nothing about hairstyles, but I could get a loan from the bank and back the opening of a beauty parlor. From boxing champ to beauty stylist.

She agreed we'd be partners, my newly acquired bankroll and her expertise. We'd call it Castro and O'Farrell Beauty Parlor after we found an empty store in a good location on Southern Blvd., in the Bronx, which we did. I thought the combination of names, one Spanish and one Irish, would attract every woman in the neighborhood.

The best laid plans etc., etc., didn't quite work out. After one year of pitiful customer boycotting I was told by one of the few customers we had, "I hate to tell you this, but people see the two names above your parlor, and the Spanish only focus on the O'Farrell and shy away, and the Americans see Castro and figure they have to speak Spanish, therefore, they go elsewhere."

Damn, and I figured the opposite would happen. I was sure we'd capture half the Bronx. Dumb Irishman strikes again!

But we were able to sell it after the first year, and I was able to pay off my bank loan.

◆ ◆ ◆

Part of my income was augmented by a summer job teaching boxing to kids eight to twelve years old in a summer school in Harlem.

Some of the older boys watched and asked if they could join. I brought them to a CYO gym, the one in which Marciano trained, and entered them in the Golden Gloves. One reached the finals at MSG and another the semi-finals, but no championship. I really became possessed to train and manage a champion, a world champion.

Enter Manny Gonzalez. Manny was an extremely handsome, tall, thin, twenty nine year old hustler, but hustler in a benign sense. He owned a bar a few blocks from my garden apartment and we became good friends, probably because he beat me at checkers for a dollar a game whenever I had time to stop by "Manny's," a name that frightened no one away.

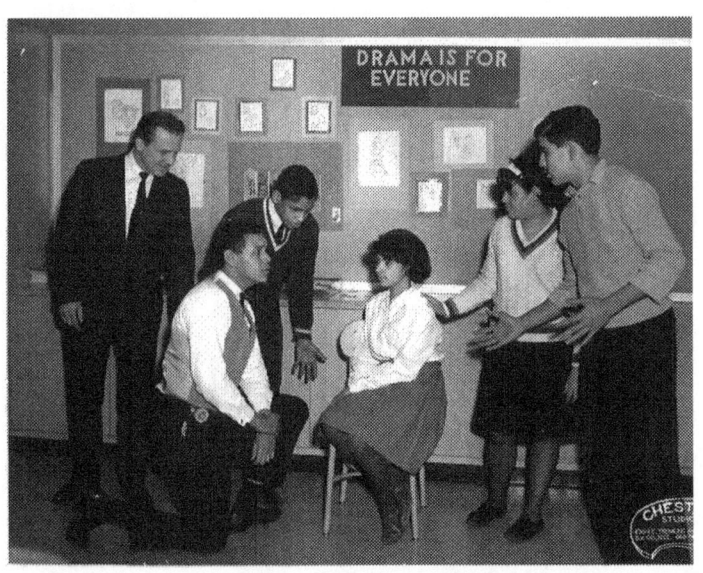

What are you asking me for? I never had an actor's role in my life!

People from his hometown in Puerto Rico sent Jose Gonzalez, (no relative) a middleweight fighter, to Manny to see what he could do to help Jose. Manny immediately took out a manager's license, although he knew nothing about managing, and became Jose's manger!

Jose was a terrific fighter in Puerto Rico and progressed even more under the tutelage of a Spanish trainer, Victor Valle, former fighter-a-la-"little" Charlie Goldman, Marciano's trainer. I was saving Manny and Jose for a later idea.

In the meantime, I had taken out a lease on a nightclub on the shore of Lake Ronkonkoma, a club that only opened during the summer season. Two other teachers in my Jr. High School 60 wanted in, so the three of us became partners. More about that later.

I still had to augment my teacher's salary. Our nightclub, "The Paradise Inn" wasn't opening for another month, and teaching boxing at night school in mid-Manhattan was right up my alley. It was so good, the N.Y. Times and Daily News decide to put my picture, story also, on the front page. But the headlines read, "Teacher Knifed in Back," with my picture under the headline, and alongside the story. Tough way to hit the front page.

A very unruly teen-ager was carrying on and busting up the basement of the school to the extent that I was called over to stop him and throw him out. As I attempted to do this he pulled a knife out of his pocket and stabbed me twice in the back. It happened in less than seconds and he took off, running like an Olympian, and I was left with blood pouring down two knife wounds in my back.

We were in the basement and I had to walk up a flight of stairs to get to the main office. I hurried into the office where three people were at their desks working.

I walked in and yelled, "Get two towels, quick." They looked at me puzzled, as I was facing the three of them and they couldn't see my back.

"Damn it," I continued, "I've been stabbed in the back." I turned around and showed them the continuous stream of blood.

Immediately, two of them ran and handed me the towels. "Not me, you! Press the towel in the top wound, to the first. As hard as you can. Pressure, pressure." To the second toweler I yelled, "Same for you, there's a wound right by my kidney. Push in, harder, harder!"

The third person sat at her desk stunned in disbelief. "Call an ambulance right now, or do you want me to dial for it myself?" I was nasty, probably my displaced anger at the knifer.

The ambulance came in 5 minutes and I walked into it and lay down, the blood having stopped because of the intense pressure I kept insisting on. As I lay there one of the ambulance workers, asked, "Do you want a priest?"

"Don't worry, I'll make it," came out of my stupid mouth. "Just get me to a hospital. If the doctors screw up, *THEN* call the priest."

We made the hospital around 145th Street in 5 minutes, and I was put on a slab of sorts. During the 5 minute ride a severe pain crossed my chest and would-n't retreat. Damn, I get knifed in the back and a pain runs across my chest. My body had it backwards.

The two doctors at the hospital who were now looking at me as I lay there began a conversation.

"You ever seen a blue streak like this?" said one, to his cohort.

"Beats me. Stabbed in the back and the whole chest has a blue streak across it."

"Will you two art admirers do something," I piped. "This hurts like Hell." They did. They had me sent to a room. I guess they wanted to shut me up! I was a consummate pain in the butt to the doctors, *BUT IT HURT!*

The T.V. cameras from the networks were in the room and reporters were shouting out questions. My mind was like a bullet and I forgot the pain. Every answer I gave to T.V. had a line such as, "When I left the "Paradise Inn" at Lake Ronkonkoma this morning"…or "I'm just anxious to get back to my nightclub, "The Paradise Inn" ad infinitum, till even the photographers were getting sicker than I, aware that I was just plugging my nightclub.

Our nightclub got a million dollars publicity and I was feeling no pain until three men in suits, shirts and ties walked into the room. I could tell by their bearing who they were. Board of Education officials. When the reporters and T.V. cameras left the madhouse the three men approached my bed.

"We're from the Board of Education," they announced. It was as if a triumvirate of little Caesars was announcing their royalty.

I nodded. They didn't ask how I was or how I felt. Their next words were, "Did you do anything to provoke the boy?" They never explained to me what one does to have a knife plunged into his back. *Twice!*

"I told him he had to leave."

"That's all?"

"That's all."

They seemed satisfied and left. In the background were two men in suits. They introduced themselves as detectives and said, "We have good leads. If we get him during the night can we wake you up to identify him?"

"Absolutely," and they dashed out. Less than one hour later they were back with a fifteen-year-old in tow.

"Is this the fellow?"

The whole incident with the knifing was less than ten seconds and I really did-n't recognize the alleged perpetrator standing between them. I started to shake my head "no." Then I stopped midway in the negative headshake and said to their prisoner, "Why did you do it?"

"Because you said you were going to throw me out," came the answer.

"That's the guy. I'd recognize him among a million faces," I lied. He hung his head as the detectives took his hands and handcuffed him.

Weeks later when the detectives were taking me to his sentencing they con-fronted me in the police car as we traveled. "You were about to say no, weren't you?" They had spotted the beginning of a "no" headshake.

"Fellows," I said, "he convicted himself." "He described what happened and his part in it and made the admission. Case closed."

The two detectives laughed and one handed the other a five-dollar bill. "We made a bet that you trapped him. I don't think my partner saw the beginning of your negative headshake, so it cost him five. Want to join the force?" We all laughed until we got to the courtroom.

It wasn't so funny there. The young prisoner was standing in front of the judge. The judge asked him, "Jose, weren't you in front of me last month?"

"Yes Sir" was the reply.

"Oh, you didn't say Sir to me last month. I'm glad to see you've improved." I almost fell off the bench upon which I was seated.

Improved? Attempted murder showed improvement? The judge gave him six months, and smiled at him cordially. Wasn't that sweet? Any questions about how I feel toward Liberal judges? Or am I being too hard on the mothers? Perhaps I was lucky the judge didn't sentence me for getting in the way of Jose's knife. Obstruction of murder, you know. I'm lucky he didn't sentence me to one year. I did get in the way twice.

My back healed, although they told me the first wound was one-quarter inch away from my kidney.

The "Paradise Inn" was a lot quieter that summer, no fights, no knifings, close to no nothing. We broke even, more or less and returned to school in September after shutting down the nightclub till next season.

One-month later while I was back at school teaching an English class, a mon-itor came in with a note from Lydia Stein, the school secretary. Everyone loved Lydia for her helpfulness and ever-pleasant good humor. The note had an urgency about it. It implored me to leave the class right away and come to the office. Immediately. I raced out of the classroom, my mind racing even faster. I had dropped Anne Marie off at school, Jimmy had not been born yet, what could it be?

I raced down five flights of stairs, two at a time, and my mind came up with nothing. As I reached the floor where the office was located Lydia Stein came running out of the office and ran toward me with a panicked look on her face. As I reached her I said, "The nightclub burned down." She was open mouthed.

"How did you know," she exclaimed.

"I didn't know. The words just came out of my mouth. My mind had been a blank as I ran down here. I couldn't figure, so I stopped trying. The words just flew when I saw you."

"ESP" we chimed in unison as though we had been practicing for weeks. Lydia was a believer too. We both cracked up, but my crack up was a lot shorter when a depressing thought hit me.

Lydia took one look at my face and said, "What, what else is the matter?"

"We have no insurance," I moaned.

"Nothing?"

"No, we figured we'd only hold The Paradise Inn a short time and insurance was unbelievably high."

"So you gambled?"

"We gambled and we lost," I said, as my moan became resignation, a resigned gambler's signature to a loss. "I'll tell the other two guys," I said as I realized I was the one who voted against insurance. Can't say I was the dumb Irishman because John Bailey (Irish) voted with me and Dave Alterman (Jewish) voted for insurance. You'd have thought the Jewish partner would have talked us into an insurance policy. He was supposed to be the smart one.

"That damn landlord," I muttered as I walked away.

"You mean the landlord?" Lydia started saying as I walked away. She realized what I was thinking vis-à-vis the landlord.

"Who knows?" I interrupted. "Remember Thomas Aquinas. Man is more inclined toward evil, rather than good. Could be anything, but I always lean toward the great philosopher." She heard me, shook her head, and returned into her office a simpler but wiser human being.

We took a ride out to Lake Ronkonkoma that weekend to see the remains. Not a rock left upon a rock. We didn't bother meeting with the landlord. Hostility was reigning.

◆ ◆ ◆

Back to Manny Gonzalez's bar. No more checkers, just a few beers and conversation.

I asked him about Jose Gonzalez, his new and first fighter. As a middleweight of 160 pounds he had won all his fights in New York and was really on his way. As we spoke about Manny's fighter, I began to take inventory of my own future and that of my family, which included a newly born son, Jimmy. Little Jim had passed his second birthday.

No, damn it, his third birthday. After the third beer I decided when the young tyke was four I would take him to the gym. Not to train, just to meet some of the fighters like Emile Griffith who was now Welterweight Champion, and others.

As I worked my way through my personal inventory I had to ask myself what do I do best and what do I do poorly. The poorly came first and it took two more beers to go through the list. Beating Manny at checkers was first on the list. The others only caused me to be disingenuous about my defects, so I figured I'd better get to the affirmative aspects of my persona and past.

Teaching, fighting, theatre, producing and one more beer and I just might put presidential candidate on the list. I went home, but something was gnawing at me, and it wasn't the alcohol.

A few years passed, Jimmy was growing, and I needed money badly. Then it hit me. Jose was now what they call "Idolo" in Puerto Rico. Emile Griffith was still world champion. Although Jose outweighed Emile, they could fight an over-the-weight fight, which means if the welterweight champ, Emile, weights in over 147 pounds it is not a championship fight, simply a regular ten round fight. Jose, who had the nickname "Monon", was a middleweight, weighing close to 160 pounds, had a huge weight advantage.

This advantage could conceivably persuade Manny to agree to a fight at Bithorn Stadium, that, and a good payday and a free trip to Puerto Rico, round trip.

I called Manny and explained my idea. I would promote a fight, Griffith versus Gonzalez. He had everything to gain and nothing to lose. If Jose lost he would be losing to a champion, never a shame. If he won, his star would be a shooting star, albeit he did have a weight advantage. Manny Gonzalez agreed. One half of this production was set. "Now I have to get Emile and his manager, Gil Clancy," I said out loud.

Little Jim, now closing in to the age of five, was sitting close to the phone and had met and become friendly with Emile, his idol now, piped up, "What's this about my man Emile, Daddy?"

"He's your man, now?"

"You bet. When you took me to the gym he played with me."

"Well, I'm trying to get Emile to fight Jose Gonzalez in Puerto Rico," I replied.

"But you were just talking to Manny Gonzalez. Is Manny Jose's father?" little Jim asked.

"No, his manger," I answered.

My son thought for a moment and asked, "Is everybody in Puerto Rico named Gonzalez?" I laughed and said, "No Jim, it just seems that way."

"I don't know any other kid named O'Farrell," he countered.

"I'll find you one," I howled.

"You confuse me, Daddy," was his answer.

"Jim," I said, "sit by me and bring me luck." He jumped up and down, scraped over a chair, and said, "Oh boy. Now I'm in it, too."

I called Griffith's manager, Gil Clancy, and he agreed to the fight, if it would be held in October. He insisted on October.

"The deal's closed Jim," I told my son, "but there are two things I'm worried about."

"What?" said a sympathetic face.

"Hurricanes and money," was the answer. My son ran quickly to the window and put his hand out. "It's not raining, and there's no hurricane," he said.

"But the hurricane season is in October," I told him. He frowned momentarily, and then brought up the topic of school.

"You have to teach school in October," he reminded me.

"I can get a sabbatical," I said.

"What's that?"

"It's when they give you time off for a few months."

"Instead of starting school, I could get a sabbatical," he rattled off.

"Sabbaticals are only for teachers," I told him.

"You guys get all the luck," he pouted.

"Then there's the money problem," I informed him.

"I saved twenty dollars," he said. "You can have it all."

"Thanks, buddy," I said, but I'm going to need a lot more."

"How much?" he queried.

"Well," I started. "Griffith gets $12,500 and Jose gets $10,000."

"How much is a thousand? More than my twenty dollars?" he queried.

"A lot. Then there's plane fare, hotel expenses, and other expenses. But now that I think of it I can get the plane and hotel comped," I said half to Jimmy and half to myself.

"What's comped," he asked.

Emile Griffith, World Champion, Peter Lopez, me, and my wife, Maria.

"A famous champion like Emile doesn't have to pay for hotel rooms and airplane tickets. They're glad to let famous champions and their entourage in for free because they get good publicity out of it." I answered.

"What's an entourage?" he managed.

Anne Marie bust through the door at that moment and said, "Are you bugging Daddy?"

"We are having a business meeting," Jim replied, one-upping his sister.

"I have to call the stadium in Puerto Rico and get a date for the fight," I said, which I did. When I finally hung up after conversing with the stadium administrator, I shouted with joy "October 5th, it's a go."

A confused Anne Marie wanted to know what was happening. I explained and my bright little girl understood. She was accustomed to her father's adventures.

"And it's going to be during the hurricane season," Jimmy shouted, "but there won't be a hurricane because Dad's birthday is October 4th and God wouldn't send any hurricanes till after it's all over. Maybe October 6th, but not before," said my little peacock. Oh, he was so proud. "Anytime you need me Dad I'll sit right beside you." He walked to the door, opened it and said, "If you need me, I'll be outside playing with the kids. I'm always available." and he winked a knowing wink, smiled and closed the door.

The fight came off as planned October 5th, no rain, and Bithorn Stadium was three quarters filled. The stadium seated sixteen thousand people and we figured there were about twelve thousand butts in the seats. Griffith won the decision.

When I went to the main office they handed me a piece of paper that said the attendance was 8,668 with a take of forty four thousand dollars. My expenses came to forty thousand, consequently my profit was four thousand dollars. Had I been taken! But everybody has to make a living, and my profit told me that I could accomplish after all. I felt this was just the beginning.

As we were counting the money the door to the office burst open. It was Manny Gonzalez. His usually pale face was in a rage. He was yelling and screaming in a maniacal solo.

"We were robbed, I can't believe it," he screamed, talking to no one in the room, just venting his anger at the whole group standing and milling about. I happened to be looking at the sheet in my hand that read only eight thousand plus people were in the stands. Manny's entrance and my disbelief that there were only eight thousand plus people attending the fight coincided.

"It certainly looks like it to me," I vented, though not with the vehemence that Jose's manager displayed. He stopped for a hurried moment and asked, "You thought Jose won the fight too?"

"Oh," I replied, "I thought you were talking about the attendance."

"Screw the attendance," Manny spewed. "I'm talking about the fight. Jose won almost every round." A typical manager's complaint when his fighter loses the decision, but this manager was hot headed and wouldn't stop his ranting.

I tried to quiet him down, but he wouldn't be stopped. "Manny," I said, "I offered to bring Rocky Marciano here to Puerto Rico to referee the fight, but you said you would pack up and cancel everything unless there were three Spanish judges. Marciano had agreed to come and I had to call him back and tell him there had to be three Spanish judges. In fact, I had to apologize profusely."

At that moment, I noticed the sports editor of the San Juan Star, Pete Anderson, had entered the room, so without pointing him out I said to the irate manager, "I have to warn you, there is a reporter in the room, so why don't you quiet down?"

I felt it was my obligation to warn Manny, yet the San Juan Star Editor was entitled to hear everything that was going on as long as he was allowed entrance into the room. Not only did Manny not stop his hysterics, but he then came out with the exclamation that was sure to make headlines and stories throughout all of the country.

"I Will Never Let Jose Gonzalez Fight in Puerto Rico Again," was the sport's headline in the San Juan Star. The follow up story told of the hotheaded antics displayed by the manager and the oath not to let the idol of Puerto Rico return. Manny was true to his red-hot words. All of the fighter's future fights were either in New York, or elsewhere in the States.

But out of perversity occasionally came some good. As the boxing card underneath the main event had unfolded, my eye caught sight of a four round fighter, named Carlos "Teo" Cruz. He was a true machine gunner, a non-stop fighter who easily defeated his opponent.

I knew I was looking at a future champion, and I was determined to bring him to New York and develop him.

I made a deal with his Puerto Rican manager to buy half his contract and bring Teo and his wife back here where I could sharpen his edges, i.e. teach him certain moves that would make him a complete fighter.

"Teo" came willingly and finally fought in Madison Square Garden where only the creams of the crop perform. His wife gave birth, her second, in a Manhattan hospital, but she was lonesome for her mother. They decided to return to San Juan, Mildred, Teo and their two children.

Meanwhile, the lightweight champion's manager "Honest" Bill Daley contacted me and asked me, "Jim, tell me the truth. Can Teo beat Carlos Ortiz, my lightweight champion?"

"Ortiz is a better fighter," I answered him. "Your fighter beats Teo, except for one thing."

"What's that?"

"Ortiz doesn't take training and conditioning as well as he should. The women love him, and he likes to party. Pound for pound Carlos Ortiz is one of the greatest lightweights of all time and should beat Teo, but I have to warn you, Teo never stops fighting, bell to bell."

"I'm not worried about my champ's condition," Honest Bill asserted.

They fought for the lightweight championship and Teo actually knocked Carlos down in the second round, the only time Teo had ever knocked anyone down, and went on to win the championship by decision. The Lightweight Champion of the World. My dream.

It was clear Ortiz was not in shape and "Honest" Bill did not do his job. To this day, I believe Carlos Ortiz was one of the all-time greats.

Tragedy struck not too long afterwards. Teo, although living in P.R. with his wife, had family in Santo Domingo, his country of birth. He took his wife, Mildred and their two children to a cousin's wedding in Santo Domingo, a half hour plane ride.

After the wedding, on the trip home to Puerto Rico, the plane went down. There was not one survivor. I'm sure God shook Teo's hand as Carlos "Teo" Cruz entered heaven. I hope the good Lord threw in "Well done, my son."

The partial success in San Juan, (and I say partial because I never found out how the extra few thousand "customers" found seats without paying) confirmed my view that producing and promoting were my strong points.

◆ ◆ ◆

Jacobo Morales, Spanish T.V. star and producer had been a dear friend of mine for years. Jacobo had been nominated for the Academy Award as "best producer of a foreign film," but he didn't win the award. "Jimmy" he has since told me "I didn't expect to win the Academy Award, but it was really a great thrill sitting next to these great producers."

That was modest Jacobo. His rise from T.V. writer, to actor, to film producer made no impression on him, and his various successes he took in stride. He has been the same every-man as the first day I met him, yet there is not one person in Puerto Rico who has not heard of this idealistic genius.

After the Griffith fight we had lunch where he introduced me to paella, rice with various types of seafoods. During the lunch he mentioned the name Pin Aguayo.

"Pin is a strange name," I said. Jacobo laughed and said, "You have some strange names in the States. Pin has been promoting fights in Santo Domingo. You should meet with him and perhaps you two can promote in Santo Domingo," he suggested.

It sounded like a good idea, and I made it a point to meet Pin. He was a very carefree individual, amazing me with his relaxed, easy-going outlook on life. We hit it off well, and we decided we'd promote together. He'd find a "name" Dominican fighter and I'd bring a fighter from the states, one who couldn't possibly win. That way we'd be making a Dominican "Idolo." It wasn't that the fight would be fixed, just that the American fighter would be inferior to his Dominican opponent.

The day of the fight arrived and ticket sales were brisk. It looked like a sunny beginning. All weigh-ins are held at noon the day of the fight to assure that one fighter does not weigh more than the contract provides.

Each fighter weighed-in satisfactorily, and everyone left the Commissioner's office and returned to their abodes. I was staying at a nice hotel ten miles out of the center of town. It was one o'clock in the afternoon and I sat by the poolside having just finished my lunch.

"Paging Mr. O'Farrell, paging Mr. O'Farrell," came an announcement over the loudspeaker. I was sure it was Pin telling me how ticket sales were increasing this day of the fight. I quickly went into the lobby, a really large lobby. I approached the desk and told them my name.

"You have a telephone call, Sir. The phone is over there by the pool windows."

I picked up the phone and said "Jim O'Farrell speaking."

"Jeemy," it was Pin.

"Hi, Partner" I beamed.

"Jeemy, there's a revolution."

"A revolution, where?"

"Here," came a despondent voice. I looked out the window and saw people swimming and splashing in the water.

"Pin, there's no revolution. Everybody's laughing and playing in the pool."

"There's a television set in your lobby," Pin said. Santo Domingo was his playground and he could tell you every inch of every hotel. "Turn it on."

I looked about, saw the T.V., ran and turned it on. "We have taken over the government," came this commanding voice. The picture was a blank. Then came the sound of machine gun fire, sporadic but distinct.

"Stay in your houses and do not resist," the voice continued, followed by the machine gun fire again. I ran to the telephone my mind racing madly, wildly, telling myself think, think, think.

"Pin, I heard it, but I have an idea."

"An idea, what?"

"When the government troops show up at our fight tonight we can put the troops on one side of the ring, and then we put the rebels on the other side."

"Jeemy, now I believe all Americans are crazy!" and he hung up the phone.

Later that day an American official came to our hotel and told the patrons a bus would arrive in the morning and take everyone to another hotel. Another bus would be waiting and American Marines would escort them to a ship, which would take everyone to Puerto Rico, and finally we would be flown back to the United States. I went to my room and attempted to make a collect phone call to home, only to be informed by the telephone operator that it would take a couple of hours to get through to New York.

I packed slowly hoping the operator would get through soon. After two hours my phone rang, I picked it up and the operator told me, "I'm getting through now." After four rings the phone was picked up and the operator quickly said, "I have a collect call from a Mr. O'Farrell."

"He's not here." It was Jimmy, and he hung up the phone right away.

The operator reported to me, "I don't think he understood me. It sounded like a little boy."

"It was my son," I said, "and is he going to get it when I get home. He's never allowed to pick up the phone."

"I can try again, but it will probably take another two hours. It's getting worse." she offered.

"Never mind, but thank you anyway. If you read about a young boy being murdered in New York, please forget about this phone call." She laughed as I hung up the phone and took a slug of rum and coca cola, my only drink since I had arrived at the hotel.

Jacobo Morales, actor and T.V. personality discussing theatre with me.

Jacobo's wife, Blanca, me, and Jacobo dining and discussing their
next film production.

The next morning at seven thirty a bus was in the front of the hotel, and all of the hotel's occupants boarded, including yours truly. We arrived at an even larger hotel ten minutes later. The lawn of this hotel was filled with other Americans sprawled on the grass in front.

As I disembarked I spotted Pin Aguayo lying on the grass, soaking up the sun. "Jeemy," he said as I knelt, then lay next to him.

"Any more bright ideas," he giggled softly. A twenty four year old fellow was patronizing me, but he had every right to do so.

"At least I was thinking," I defended myself.

"Jeemy, do me a favor," he said. "Don't think no more."

As we were conversing and getting a quick tan, four soldiers with machine guns came running and spread themselves out surrounding the hotel. The leader of this group ran over to Pin and said, "Hey amigo, give me a cigarette."

"Jorge" Pin replied as he handed over a cigarette and lit it for the soldier. "Como esta?"

"Bueno," was the answer as the soldier ran to his position taking two puffs on the way.

"Who was that?" I asked.

"Capitan Jorge Mendez," was the answer. "He runs the whorehouse in the center of town. He's a good guy."

As Pin was finishing his sentence machine gun fire spit out from the guns of Jorge and his soldiers. "My God," I yelled. Pin never moved. He just kept enjoying the sun. More machine gun fire, almost non-stop aimed at the hotel.

"Whom are they shooting at?" I asked.

"Nobody," Pin said. "They're just showing off for the Americans. Nobody is in the hotel."

"Yeah," was my answer, midst more stray bullets. "I'm getting the Hell out of here," as I jumped to my feet and started running to the front door of the hotel. I know my feet were moving because I got to the door, but during my run I looked down and my legs appeared frozen. "Feet go, go," I urged, and they picked up the pace. When I reached he door I notice a pack of people who had been on the grass following me. My first fear was a mad rush could lead to people trampling trying to squeeze through the narrow door. Turned out it was a side door I had reached, not the front. But they all followed me.

"Walk, do not run," I kept repeating in a loud authoritative voice, as they hurriedly filed by while I kept holding the door open. My mind flashed to school fire drills and the danger of injury because of panic. I held the door open yelling over and over "Walk, damn it walk. Some cursed me as they walked by others threw out a quick "thanks."

I spotted Pin calmly talking to his Capitan. They were probably discussing the whorehouse. The soldiers disappeared as quickly as they came, and three buses pulled up in front of the hotel. The people were then told the buses would take them to a ship headed for Puerto Rico. Trailing the last bus was a Dominican troop van with armed soldiers being used as a rear escort.

The people then filed back and approached their new means of transport. American officials told them to board the buses single file. A long, long line formed, and I, in sheer detestation and stubbornness regarding lines, waited till the buses were practically filled.

As the people passed me one man and his wife, in their late twenties, said to me, "You're with the C.I.A. aren't you?" I smiled knowingly, said nothing, and felt ten feet tall. What the Hell, could I disabuse them of having met an agent, a C.I.A. agent, involved in a revolution? What a story for them to tell back home!

The buses filled up with Americans and others quicker than I anticipated, and I found myself racing to catch the last bus, much like a New Yorker at 42nd Street, but I missed it, I missed it.

The transportation moved on and I was left, figuring I had better learn to speak Spanish. One last hope, the rear echelon truck, the one armed with government troops, assigned to follow and protect the transporters had just started its motor.

"Commandante, commandante," I yelled running to the truck. "Me, me," I yelled at the soldier standing outside the truck over-seeing everything.

When I reached him he said one word to me, "Money." He was holding me up for American dollars.

I kept my money in my right pocket, so I quickly pulled out my left pocket and turned it inside out, two, maybe three times.

"Nada," I said, "Nothing, I'm broke, good buddy." I put my hand on his right shoulder. "I have to travel on your truck with your soldiers. You're the back up."

He seemed to take pity, and said in perfect English, "O.K., get in." I climbed aboard his vehicle and Wow. Twenty soldiers seated all at attention, ten on one side facing ten on the other side, rifles in their hands, and two young teen-agers facing each other, handcuffed and sitting on the floor.

I squeezed in between two soldiers hoping they would not think I was an enemy. What if the two handcuffed boys sitting on the floor said "Hola" (Hello), I'd be dead. The boys said nothing and the soldiers sat stone faced staring straight ahead.

"You comfortable, Senor?" the commandante asked with his plastic grin.

"Very," I answered, scared to death. The buses and escorts reached the ship and we boarded without incident.

A well-built man in his mid twenties approached me and said, "They took over the T.V. station first. That's what they are supposed to do. Seize and control the propaganda. That's half the battle." The man was obviously Spanish, judging by his accent, even though his English was perfect.

"What about all that phony machine gunning?" I asked.

"That wasn't phony," he said. "They were looking for us but we weren't there."

I *did not* want to know who "us" and "we" were, so I excused myself and told him I was going to get something to eat. He patted me on the back with his hand, which did not have a knife in it. Paranoid? Who me? Never heard of Paranoia.

Soon we docked in Puerto Rico, flew to New York, and met every cameraman in the media. There went my C.I.A. cover. Friends in my neighborhood looked at me quizzically. Even they had suspicions.

Not long after I returned home, the most tragic event in my life occurred. May this never happen to any reader, or for that matter, anyone with a young child.

It was a Saturday afternoon. Our garden apartment was on the first floor overlooking the backyard where the children played on weekends and after school.

Jimmy's mom and Anne Marie went downtown shopping for dresses. I'm a nervous Nellie when it comes to little children. The kids were noisily playing tag, and doing all the things that five to eight year old children do. I looked out the window every fifteen minutes and checked that they were all there. I was the *only* parent attending to the childish madhouse in the back.

Not only that, I would leave the apartment on the half hour, walk to where they were, sort of hide, as I watched and counted. I didn't want the kids to see me and think they couldn't enjoy themselves.

At one point, Jimmy came into the house and asked if he could have a quarter. I assumed they were trading or selling comic books or other paraphernalia, so I gave it to him without hesitation.

Ten minutes later I sneaked to my observation post to count the kids. One was missing. It was Jimmy. He had been wearing a flaming red cowboy outfit, but he wasn't there.

I ran to the group and asked, "Where's Jimmy?"

Toddy, a five year old from across the street answered, "Oh he must be the kid hit by the truck." Toddy continued playing. I ran swiftly to the street and saw a crowd gathered around a tiny figure. The figure was all in red. Jimmy was lying unconscious surrounded by adult onlookers.

I raced the thirty yards. "Let me through," I pushed through the crowd.

"Did anyone call an ambulance?" I screamed.

"I did," someone yelled, "two minutes ago." It had just happened. Jimmy was semi-conscious, eyes closed, rolling his head slowly side to side. He was still alive. A police car, sirens screaming, screeched to a halt. An officer quickly asked, "Can we take him to a hospital?"

"No," I answered. I knew moving a body took professional handling, and I was sure it was possible to do more harm with inept movement. I knew just moving an injured person by non-professionals could cause serious internal injuries.

The crowd started screaming, "Take him now, take him now." He was still moving his head from side to side.

I waited more minutes and one of the policemen urged me to let them take him. Finally, after a minute or two, I succumbed to the crowd. "I'll pick him up," I told the officer. I cuddled his young head in one arm and used the other arm to balance his body close to mine. I knew it was no time for tears, just action. He lay in my arms in the back seat of the police car as I kept calling to him and telling him he was with me. I didn't want him to reach unconsciousness. I kept trying to keep him awake, partially conscious. One of the officers took out a bullet and handed it to me.

"Look, Jim, a real bullet. Let's play with it Buddy. Jim, try to play with Daddy." I felt I must keep him conscious. I was afraid if he became unconscious he would never return.

We reached the hospital; they took x-rays and told me his spleen had to be removed. The spleen helps fight off infections.

I said, "Do it, but then what?" They told me he would have to have sulfur every day for the next two years and that would help fight off any infections.

The night was unsleepable at the hospital as they gave me a bed. His mother came early in the evening, leaving Anne Marie with neighbors.

The next day Emile Griffith came to the hospital and finally Jimmy responded as he heard Emile's voice, and semi-consciousness began its twilight journey to full consciousness. Emile kidded with him and little Jimmy finally came to our world, fully awake. Within ten days he was home again. "Dad, I don't have to go to school now do I?" He was back. This was my Jim; but I wanted revenge.

The day after he left the hospital I went into our backyard with the red cowboy suit which I had bought him, and I burned every inch of it. It was early morning.

"*You will never hurt my son again,*" I thought, as though the truck was not involved, the driver was not involved, only the cowboy suit.

I cried a crazy, emotional, insane cry, as if I were purging what had happened and my actions would place everything back together into the real world, and put all past events into an unreal dream. I was bereft of my senses at that moment, until I saw only ashes on the ground. I sighed and walked away, thinking "let someone else clean it up. I don't want to know it existed!"

Months later Jimmy asked me if he hadn't had a red play suit once, to which I said, "I got rid of that a long time ago, Jim," and changed the subject. I could have added, "You try and rid yourself of what hurts most in life, Jim." Another unrealistic thought.

◆ ◆ ◆

As time went by my head and emotions took a rational form and I began to think of my own situation. My success with plays produced in school, all Broadway plays and musicals, were on the plus side of what I could do well. I had one plus with the production of Griffith versus Gonzalez at Bithorn Stadium in Puerto Rico, and one neutral with the revolutionary interruption in Santo Domingo.

Once again I called upon my great friend Jacobo Morales, then TV star in San Juan, Puerto Rico. I called him long distance and asked him if he could get me reservations at El Teatro Tapia, the Tapia Theatre.

"What show, what date?" he asked.

"No, no," I replied. "I mean an open date for a show which I will produce." He seemed perplexed.

I explained further. "I have in mind producing a show on Broadway, but I want to try it out first in San Juan. There is a large American population in your city, and, if they like it, I can think about bringing it to Broadway."

"What's the name of the show and who is the star?"

"There he goes again," I thought, "always the perfectionist."

"No name, no show yet, but I'll have that all accomplished within the next two months." I hoped that would assuage Jacobo.

A long silence led me to believe that I would hear the voice of Pin Aguayo saying, "Jeemy, have you gone loco?" Instead it was Jacobo saying, "I'll reserve the theater for three months from now," no incredulity, just a faithful friend undertaking what he was asked to do. He came through and had the Tapia Theatre reserved exactly three months from our conversation. Because it was Jacobo Morales the theatre did not ask for a deposit and I was on my way.

Jerry Huggard, an extremely handsome friend, heard about my plans and asked me if he could go partners with me. I agreed and once again I had a fifty-fifty partner.

Jerry searched for an original script, a comedy, and I hunted down Wendy Barrie's agent, explained my plans, and convinced him that Wendy would be the star, full title above everyone else, salary agreeable, a week in Puerto Rico, all expenses paid, first class hotel, first class everything. If all went well in San Juan, I would make every attempt to bring the show to Broadway.

Wendy had starred with Humphrey Bogart, made other movies, and was just finishing a TV afternoon show a-la-Oprah. Her television contract had just run out and she was looking for another vehicle. This might be just what she was looking for.

In the meantime Jerry, my partner, came across an original comedy entitled "Dear Old Alma Mater." I read the first act, which showed promise, and went about signing up three other performers, two men and one woman, for a cast of four. Wendy was to be the wife of James Olson, a Broadway newcomer. The other couple a boyfriend and girlfriend, who were to have dinner at Wendy's and her husband's house. From then on the plot developed into a comedy of errors.

I hired a rehearsal hall at midtown Manhattan, rehearsed for three weeks and finally departed for San Juan. I comped everyone, thereby saving plane fare, but Wendy insisted she and I sit in the first class section. She told me she wanted to go over lines with me.

The flight began with her telling me she was named Wendy after the Wendy in "Peter Pan" which had been written by her uncle, one of the Barrie's. I don't remember which one, because I always get them mixed up (and my son thinks I'm smart) but it's true. I'll take a guess now and say Phillip Barrie, but it was probably his brother (there, now I have both of them covered). Now you know where my son inherited his classic case of confusion. (Actually it was J.M. Barrie). Wendy also told me she was the women's tennis champion in New Jersey.

There was an elderly couple sitting in back of us. As they heard my seatmate tell me about being named "Wendy" after the Peter Pan Wendy the elderly lady tapped my star on her shoulder and asked, "Are you Wendy Barrie?"

Miss Barrie was obviously pleased as punch. She affirmed the question, and then the grilling began. Every question conceivable was thrown the actress's way, and she, in her outgoing manner, confirmed, re-affirmed and augmented each query with a storm of stories, information and a flood of general conversation. I could see our script-studying going out the window. Actually, I had a suspicion she had her part in the script down cold and just wanted me along as a male companion, as female actresses were wont to do. God forbid she should travel alone, when she could travel with a man ten years her junior. But this was just the first part of my adventure.

Our publicist, a fellow hired by my partner, had arranged for a columnist to be at the Hilton Hotel for our arrival. The columnist, a pretty young girl in her late twenties introduced herself and began asking questions for her women's column immediately after we arrived in the room. She worked for the San Juan star, and remembering how the Sports Editor, Pete Anderson, had plugged the Griffith fight I was ready to accommodate this young lady to the utmost, even though I was sure the first thing Wendy wanted was to take a shower, get into something comfortable, and relax. But like a true champion, tennis or otherwise, the film star was the essence of courtesy, charm and elegance. I don't know how she did it. But as I say, she was a pro. No, make that a pro's pro. As I was leaving she told me, "Tomorrow we'll go swimming." I was the only one in the room, but to make sure I sneaked a look around the room and asked in as chipper a manner as I could, "What time?" "Right after breakfast, pick me up around ten thirty." I almost saluted, but nodded my head with a meek "OK" and high-tailed it out of her room as fast as I could.

I made arrangements at the "La Concha", a nearby hotel figuring it would not be as crowded as the Hilton. My brain cells were on hold. Every film star would want as many people as possible gaping at her, and the more who gaped the more would fill the house at the theatre. It's good to be Irish, but not a dumb Irishman. But my star was not familiar with San Juan, and all she knew was that the Hilton was rated number one. For all she knew the La Concha was almost its equal, as it was only five minutes away.

When we arrived at our swimming destination the next morning I noticed the look on Wendy's face that said, "Where are all the people," but she never uttered a word. We went into the hotel, out to the swimming pool and she did her thing, which was diving off the diving board, back flips, front flips, which I'm sure, the 7 people who were seated around the pool enjoyed. The 7 clapped enthusiastically. If they hadn't applauded with such gusto I would have had to consider it a catastrophe. Oh well, what the Hell…live and learn, and try not to be a dumb Irishman.

Rehearsals started at the theater the next day, but Wendy wanted only half a day. She wanted to go into town to shop for dresses, which she would wear for the performances. She looked around for a male companion to accompany her and tell her how good she looked in the dresses she tried on. It wasn't ego now; it was truly that she wanted someone else's opinion. Her companion was chosen, guess who, even though I wasn't a fountain of information regarding what the fairer sex was wearing. Truth is, I know nothing, absolutely nothing, about fashion. If we were to go to a sport store and check out football Jerseys and boxing headgear I would have been her guy. I told her this in a voice she hadn't heard up to this time. She grabbed my arm, moved me along and laughingly said, "I'll buy you a tennis racket if you tell me what you like and what you don't like, what looks good and what doesn't go with me."

"I can't go with you." I was about to say, but cowardice was the better part of valor. All I could say was, "But I don't play tennis."

"I'll fill you in about forehand and backhand, and you'll be a star," she told me as she led me through the theatre doors and told me of a dress shop the hotel people had told her about that morning. "It's only a few blocks from here and we'll be finished in no time." Can anyone tell me how any movie star, strike that, make it any woman, is finished in 'no time'. Wendy knew what she wanted, and knew how to get it without losing an ounce of femininity and grace.

Truthfully, I had a hangover, the Goddess of all hangovers from the night before, having spent a few hours trying to figure out how I had gotten into all this, and if she tried on a barrel I would have told her it was just right, maybe a bit tight. Never tell a woman something is too tight, even a barrel. But the luck of the Irish kicked in and we walked to the dress shop and my star chatted away ever so pleasantly. The glimmerings of a deal took shape. I knew I could make this deal reach fruition. We were greeted as royalty when we entered the shop. Wendy was busy trying on dresses and getting my okay while I pulled the shop owner aside.

"Look, we can make a deal." I intoned to the owner, another lovely creature.

"Such as?" she inquired.

"Let Wendy Barrie take two dresses on loan which will be returned to you right after our one week of performances. The dresses will be cleaned and ironed as if they were never worn."

"And what do I get in return?" she asked.

"You will get a free advertisement for your dress shop and a notice in the playbill will announce that all the costumes Miss Barrie wears were provided by you personally."

"What's a playbill?"

Dear Lord must I. In language a kindergarten student could understand I explained, "Everyone who enters the theatre for each performance is handed a playbill. The playbill tells who the actors are and what part they are playing and how many acts and scenes are in the play. Also, and here's where you and your dress shop come in, the playbill will have a full page advertising your shop and the fact that you personally helped Miss Barrie choose her costumes which in this case are the two dresses she seems to like. And it won't cost either of us a penny."

"That's great. Take the dresses," she literally screamed.

My hangover was gone and I escorted Wendy back to the Hilton while she chatted about backhands and forehands and did I really like the dresses.

"Wendy" I told her, "this was a great afternoon. I'm so glad you picked me to go with you."

That's called blarney.

◆　◆　◆

Rehearsals for the week went well. Miss Barrie, which I called her now for the purpose of establishing a little more formality, which in turn established a little more distance, knew her lines and her marks to perfection. She had everything down cold. The scenes in which she kissed James Olsen, playing her husband were wifely, and the other two actors, Larry Webber and Patricia Parker, gorgeous ingénue, could hardly wait for opening night.

It came, and every seat in the house was filled. There was one I wished had been empty, and that seat was occupied by the critic of my favorite paper, The San Juan Star. How many shows does a critic in a city with one theatre get to review each year? The audience was made up of all English speaking people who enjoyed the comedy to a reasonable extent.

The critic's review the next day was made up of negative clichés, such as "It looked like a Chinese fire drill," ad infinitum. I think he had written his review long before he saw the play. Believe me there wasn't one Chinese character in the play.

We completed the week we signed to do, but I could see Broadway was not on the horizon, which I told the cast of four at the end of the week. The one event I will never forget was the very opening of the play when the curtain went up. The setting was the living room of a lovely house which furniture I had bargained for, much the same way I obtained Wendy's dresses.

As the curtain rose, Miss Barrie walked into the room with her arms full with packages. Two steps into the room on stage she dropped one of the packages, *definitely not a part of the play*. Everything fell out. She picked up the cornflakes, butter, bread and everything else on the floor, and placed every single item on the table. She then ad-libbed something about this damn shopping. Her ad-lib was as genuine as any housewife dropping a bag after a long day's shopping. If I had thought of those lines I would have put them in myself. She just went on as if it had happened a hundred times before, and she didn't miss a beat. My heart jumped up to my skull when the cornflakes popped out and I almost fainted when the bread came falling away. She not only saved the beginning, she made it a part of every day life.

Yours truly made the next faux pas. You have to understand this, and any sympathy you can muster up I will greatly appreciate. This faux pas happened because I was born two days early. Everything I have done, I have done early, *a lot early*. Never invite me to your house for dinner, for I will arrive right after lunch. It seems I think the world will end if I'm not early. The janitor of my high school often asked me what I was doing sitting by the door of the school ten minutes before he opened it. And I hated school. I never wanted to be there. Never!

Before the play began I stationed myself stage right against the wall just behind the curtain. In that way the audience would never see me, and I would be able to hold the script in my hand just in case one of the actors forgot a line and I was able to whisper the line loud enough for the actor to hear, but low enough to escape the ears of the audience.

Right across from me at stage left was the stagehand positioning himself also against the wall so he could not be seen. He was to watch me.

His job was simply to open and close the curtain at my signal, nothing more nothing less. He was Spanish and spoke a good bit of English, however, I thought it best to arrange a series of signals. It was to be thusly. When I raised my hand high above my head and brought the hand down quickly, that was his signal to open the curtain. The same held true for closing the curtain.

As the act proceeded and was a few lines from the end, I would raise the same hand high above my head, and, at the closing line of the act I would slam my raised hand down to my side, and he would close the curtain to the applause of the audience.

Simple, hand up, get ready. Hand down, open or close the curtain. We worked on this all week, and although his English was limited he was able to follow most of the dialogue, having heard it all week, and having worked as a team with me in unison. Actually his English was even better than I thought, as I often saw him laughing at some of the comedy lines, and goings on, as the actors spoke and pranced about the stage in what was hopefully to be hilarity.

The opening night of the show the first act worked perfectly between us. The curtain opened and closed exactly on cue. I had a great partner and any worries I had about him were quickly dispelled. At times he became hysterical at some of the lines, but after a week of listening to the dialogue, day after day, he seemed to absorb the whole play. If only the American audience reacted as he did we were on our way.

On the wall next to me was a buzzer. It was called, "the five-minute buzzer." When I buzzed, it was to alert the audience that the intermission was to be over in five minutes, and the people who had been mingling, and talking, and laughing, were to be back in their seats, waiting for the second act to begin.

Most of our patrons had been using the two bathrooms or chatting among themselves in the back of the theatre, more or less stretching their legs.

I would have none of it. If there is a five-minute buzzer you should be back in your seats in three minutes.

"Always early Jim," struck again. Two of our actors were already seated in their positions facing the audience waiting for the curtain to go up to begin their dialogue. I gave my curtain pulling cohort the signal by raising my hand and coming down with it quickly.

The stagehand seemed perplexed. He knew I had rung the five-minute buzzer, yet, as he looked at his watch, only three minutes had passed. He gave me a "What's up?" look. I became furious.

I raised my hand again and slammed it down as if I were leading a symphony orchestra. He shrugged his shoulders and raised the curtain. He felt order were orders!

The total scene wasn't exactly bedlam, but it was as close to it as you can get. Ladies and their husbands elbowed others to get to their seats. Those being elbowed griped at the lack of manners of others who in turn griped at others, ad infinitum, hardly without choice words at having been pushed, shoved, and almost trampled. The audience had begun to hate each other, which really does not bode well for the play.

My curtain cohort looked at me with one of those, "I could have told you so," looks, both his hands spread apart from his body, palms upward as if saying to the heavens, "What can I do with this damn Yankee? He's the boss!"

Patricia and Larry, the houseguests of Wendy in the play, saw the mad trample to the seats and did not begin their lines.

Larry put his head in his hands, faking a bad hangover and saying nothing. He knew it would give him a few extra seconds before he began his first line.

When he did begin his first line he came up with something like, "I knew I shouldn't have drank that much last night."

Patricia, who was new to the stage, stared a pregnant moment and finally answered, "Don't I always tell you to go easy? It's for your own good."

They carried on a dialogue, totally impromptu, about his drinking, which had absolutely nothing to do with the play, then or later.

It took the audience another minute or so to settle, not without muttering, and if my ears picked it up correctly, a bit of whispered cursing; at each other, at the play, at everything and everybody but me, the culprit.

I swore I would be late for the rest of my life. Even if the President invited me to a Presidential dinner.

When a show sinks mid part there is nothing than can save it, not even a Wendy Barrie. When the final curtain came down this fine actress took her bows from a very courteous audience. They were very friendly to Miss Barrie, slightly less so to the other members of the cast.

As the curtain came down and my star walked passed me she said loudly enough for those backstage to hear her say, "You would think the producers would have a dozen roses presented to me as the audience was applauding."

True, I had forgotten the flowers, a usual Broadway presentation at the opening of a new show.

Aw, Hell, I just wanted to get back to my hotel and figure out the easiest way to commit suicide.

I had arranged for a radio interview between Wendy and a hostess who had her own radio talk show between the hours of eleven P.M. and midnight. I had never mentioned it to Miss Barrie, as I wanted to surprise her. Her segment was only to be five to ten minutes and it would be good publicity. I skipped it, leaving the hostess high and dry.

I said to myself, "The Hell with it." I had arranged for a TV interview the week of rehearsals, which my star attended and proceeded to talk in a humorous vein about her various divorces, strictly a no-no at that time in Puerto Rico. It would have played very humorously in the states, but not in Spanish countries. I should have known this was an omen.

The next day the box office was deluged with phone calls. The review of the play had been prominently displayed on the entertainment page and our office was inundated with cancellations. If the reviewer had any self-respect he would have written it in Chinese since he was so enamored with Chinese fire drills.

As I thought back upon the cast I placated myself with the thought they all were paid handsomely, they swam and played at the various beaches in the early morning before rehearsals and show times, they had a free trip to Puerto Rico, saw the sights when possible, and got to perform in a play that stunk. I knew they could have done without the latter, but God didn't design life to be perfect. The play should have been titled "Heaven can wait," but that wouldn't have been original.

Now there was the O'Farrell family, two children and a wife. My divorce did not take place until four years after that, but at this point I was confronted with the here and now.

My partner, Jerry, was able to cover his share of the two thousand dollars still owed, but I was broke and searching my mind for some way to come up with the money, one thousand pesos.

As is usually the way an only child, me, turns to his last point of desperation. His mother. I hied myself to a Western Union Office and sent a telegram to my Mom.

I did not plead. I begged. The telegram went along the lines of "Dear Mom, things did not go exactly as I planned here in San Juan, Puerto, although the audience really enjoyed the first night performance. For some reason, which I will have to figure out, cancellations for reservations began pouring in the next morning, quite early in fact. The rest of the week the theatre was quite empty, leaving our box-office exceptionally empty. My first thought was that a bubonic plaque had overtaken this beautiful city, but the Dept. of Health assured me that no such occurrence had taken place. Consequently, I shall either have to learn fluent Spanish and get a job washing dishes in a barrio, or I shall have to request a loan from you for one thousand dollars in order to return my children and myself to New York." (She didn't like my then-wife so I thought it wiser to leave Anne's name out of the telegram.)

I continued, "I will leave it to your discretion and wisdom to decide which path we all shall follow. I know you have always wanted me to become fluent in various languages, so if you choose my working in a barrio be certain I will follow your dictates. If you decide to send the thousand I will always be grateful. Your loving son, Jim." I changed the end to, "everlastingly be grateful."

It was a lengthy and costly telegram, one that almost tore the heart out of me, but in the end it proved worth it. Believe me I sweated over every word and syllable. I would have written it on my knees if necessary.

The g. note came in the next two days with the motherly note, "Wise up, Kiddo, I'm not the Queen of England." But she did come through, as I knew she would. Momma was acerbic, but always generous.

A return home was like a vacation. Not enough to keep me still, more like a reprieve.

I dined with friends, made the rounds, played with the kids, and, of course, got restless. My back was never the same after the knife wounds so I decided to put in for disability retirement from the Board of Education. I had been teaching for twenty years; the whole milieu in schools as well as society was changing. I sought out people who were interesting.

Jack Newfield, investigative reporter for the Village Voice, and I were friends. Jack was just a notch under Bob Woodward and Carl Bernstein, the Watergate reporters. One of Jack's favorite columns was his list of the ten worst judges in New York, which he wrote annually. He was on top of everything. His main interest was politics, and Bobby Kennedy was his idol. He helped the Kennedys in many ways in New York. Mario Cuomo was one of his pet projects and his hope was to see Cuomo rise to the top. He did everything he could to be of assistance to Cuomo before Mario really started his political ascendancy.

But, above all, Jack was a fight buff. He told me the most enjoyable six hours of his life were spent watching fight films, which ranged from the nineteen forties to the seventies.

One night as we dined in a restaurant close to Madison Square Garden waiting to see the heavy weight championship fight Ali-Frazier II, Jack asked me, "Jimmy, how would you like to write for the Village Voice?" I hesitated a long moment and asked, "Write what, Jack?"

"Boxing columns," he answered.

"What makes you think I can write?" I questioned.

"When you were producing those shows at your school didn't you do some writing for the shows?"

"You know, Jack, nobody knows how much writing I did to raise all that money. You remember the plays were all Broadway shows? Well, a Broadway show runs over two hours."

"What do you mean?" he asked.

"We had the seventh, eighth, and ninth grade students coming in at three different times. Only forty-five minutes was allotted for each grade. That meant the seventh grade saw the show in forty five minutes, the eighth grade saw the show in forty-five minutes, etc."

"How did you jam two and a half hour plays into forty-five minutes?"

"I never used one original script. I knew the plots of each show and wrote the dialogue from memory," I answered.

"How did you memorize the dialogue?" he asked.

"I didn't. I knew the plots, the character, and the various happenings in the play. I more or less had the characters playing their roles according to my interpretation of the play and my dialogue."

"But if you didn't use the original scripts couldn't they have sued you. I mean, for example, 'The Music Man'. You were advertising it as 'The Music Man', yet you weren't using the original script that played Broadway, and you were not paying royalties."

"Jack, I had to condense each show to forty-five minutes as I told you, so I used O'Farrell's version of the play. As far as suing our Junior High school, can you imagine the unbelievably bad press they would get? Think of the headlines, Jack." 'Producers of Music Man Suing School Raising Thousands of Dollars Helping Indigent Minority Children,' "and the following story would generate horrible publicity. No producer wants negative publicity. Would you write the story?"

"No way,"

"Case closed."

"But you're going to write for the Village Voice?"

"Just boxing?" I queried.

"Exactly," he said.

"And only the big fights?" I threw in.

"If you want."

"How much do I get paid?"

"Two hundred dollars a column, and expenses," was Jack's answer.

"OK, finish your meal and I've got the check," I said.

"No, the newspaper gets the check. I just hired you, and that's a business expense."

We laughed and went on to Madison Square Gardens to see Ali and Frazier II, which would be the first column about which I would write. I had to have it in by Monday noon as the paper "went to bed" at that time, and was on the newsstands on Wednesdays.

A final note on Jack Newfield's passion for sports. He told me if he ever had a son he would name him Joe.

"How come Joe?" I asked. He smiled and answered, "Joe DiMaggio, Joe Louis," accenting the Joe.

We saw the fight between the two greats that night and I was reasonably relaxed. I had bet fifteen dollars on Ali with a friend. Ali won.

Not so the first meeting between Frazier and Ali three years previously. I was a nervous wreck throughout Ali-Frazier I. Ali had been away from boxing for three and a half years, having only two easy tune-ups before the fight labeled Ali-Frazier I. Joe Frazier was perpetual motion, and if you were out of boxing three and a half years you were courting disaster trying to battle the calibre of a Joe Frazier.

This all made sense to me so I took a gigantic step and found a bookie. I bet the bookie sixteen hundred dollars that Frazier would win the fight. I had to lay eight to five, which means that I was betting sixteen hundred dollars to win one thousand dollars.

The only problem was I didn't have sixteen hundred dollars! I hardly had six dollars. You can bet a bookie over the phone, and pay up time comes at the end of the week or the beginning of the next week, which ever is convenient for you.

A Beneficial Finance Company was located on Southern Boulevard in the Bronx, just three blocks away from the school in which I was teaching. I hadn't retired yet at that time.

It was almost a monthly occurrence that I would walk into the office for borrowing purposes and be greeted by many of my ex-students who worked there.

"Hi, Mr. O'Farrell, how much this month?" was always my greeting, and as more ex-students began working there it sounded like a Greek chorus in a far away play. The students, now workers, were always pleasant as I was not only their former teacher, but also one of their best customers. I have to admit it was embarrassing at first, but I got used to it.

I actually did not have enough money to see the fight at Madison Square Garden, so I did the next best thing. I went to a movie house on the Grand Concourse in the Bronx, which was showing the fight for just a few bucks, and got a seat high up in the balcony.

Muhammad Ali was, and always has been, the most popular fighter (Joe Louis a close second and Rocky Marciano a close third) not only in the United States but in the world, so it was inevitable that Don Dunphy, who was announcing the blow by blow description of the fight, would accent all the positive things that Muhammad was doing, and overlook the blows that Frazier was landing.

In the fourteenth round of the fifteen round fight, the perpetual motion little guy landed a crushing left hook to Ali's jaw that floored the idol. "Don't get up, don't get up," I screamed as loud as I could in the theatre. I could feel thousands of eyes trained on me in utter hate. Everyone in the theatre was rooting for their main man, Ali, but they hadn't bet the sixteen hundred!

Ali got up, but the ensuing fifteenth round was enough to put the fight in the victory column for Smokin Joe in my mind.

The ring announcer collected the cards, one from the referee, and one each from the two judges. "The winner," he announced, "Joe Frazier."

I left the theatre quicker than Jesse James, lest I be mobbed by those who heard me begging Ali to, "Stay down, stay down."

My reasoning for the bet was factual, not emotional, which is the way it should always be when you are betting. Ask those in the stock market.

"I was rooting for Ali," Jack told me. "How come you bet on Ali this time?" he queried.

"Fifteen dollars," I answered. "This one is going to be close, although Ali should win. But, I don't need a heart attack waiting for the decision to be announced." Ali did win the Ali-Frazier II, reversing the outcome of Frazier I.

As we walked to the Garden I told him, "You know, Jack, a referee should never judge a fight."

"Why not, he's in the ring closest to the fighters?"

I explained. "I refereed a fight once. The Kip's Bay Boy's club asked me to referee one particular fight because of my experience fighting, training, managing and promoting. They thought I would be ideal. So did I, so I agreed. I was standing in the ring going over the do's and don'ts of refereeing as the fighters entered.

Rule one: Don't stand in one place more than a second or two because you will block the view of the spectators. Keep moving. Watch for low blows. Warn the fighter who throws the low blow the first time he does it. If he lands a second low blow take one point away from him. Break clinches quickly. Often, when a fighter becomes tired he will clinch and hang on to his opponent. Also, when a fighter is hurt he will try to hang on to his opponent to give himself time to recover. My mind raced through the do's and don'ts as I waved both fighters to the center of the ring to receive my instructions.

The bell rang for the first round and both fighters moved to the center of the ring to begin the fight.

I remembered rule number one and began moving around the fighters to accommodate the customers, particularly those in the first and second rows. There were many clinches in the first round and I had warned the fighters in the pre-fight instructions not to hit on the break, that is, as I was breaking the clinch. The fighters were to step back as I put my arms in-between them. I wanted clean breaks. The fighting continued.

The bell rang ending the first round and both fighters returned to their corners. No rules were broken and I did my job without incident.

Oh, oh, who won the round? I had no idea! I was so intent on making sure all the rules were followed I paid no attention to the punches that landed cleanly, what effect they had, which boxer threw the most, just the simple things that decide a fight.

Was I in trouble. I had a scorecard in my back pocket and looked at it blankly. If I put a check next to fighter A's name maybe I'd be cheating fighter B. Vice Versa, a check next to B could cheat A. If I called it a draw, even, maybe I'd be cheating…What do I do? The minutes rest gave me time to think. My first thought was get the Hell out of the ring and forget the whole thing. No, that would have been cheating everybody.

My second thought was the answer. I casually walked over to the first judge and asked him quietly, "Whom did you have winning the round?"

"Fighter A," he proclaimed in a very assertive manner. A manner that indicated there should be no doubt.

Then I walked over to the second judge. If he said Fighter B…. well, I couldn't flip a coin in the center of the ring. The answer became clear immediately. If judge number one said A, and judge number two said B then I would call the first round a draw, even.

I approached judge number two and asked him the same question I asked number one. "Whom did you have?' His answer was such a relief. "Fighter A easily." I nodded knowingly as if in total agreement.

I scribbled on my scorecard the name of Fighter A. All three of us were now in agreement.

One round the two judges were in disagreement, so I called it a draw. Fighter A was so far ahead it didn't matter. He was awarded the decision. Couldn't he have knocked out B and helped me clear my conscience?

"And Jack, that was the end of my career as a referee."

"Maybe that's why we get such lousy decision," Newfield said derisively. But Jack was derisive about a lot of things.

Jack Newfield died a few years ago, fighting the good fight as he had so often done in all his columns. Those who knew him best will remember him, a true fighter in every sense of the word.

Now I was writing for the Village Voice, an enjoyable bit of work, but not without its hazards.

◆ ◆ ◆

A memorable event took place in Las Vegas just before the George Foreman-Ron Lyle fight. At that time it had been rumored that Foreman was a nasty fellow. He used all 226 pounds of his person to bully people, according to those who knew him best. I didn't know if he was getting a bad rap from jealous rivals, or he really was a nasty human being. His personality was his business. A sports writer's business was to report how he did in the ring.

I was informed a press conference was to be held the next morning in the forum, which was to hold the fight.

I was there early along with seven or eight other sports writers. Foreman arrived a few minutes after us with his manager and trainer and a few friends, otherwise known as hanger-ons. Nobody seemed to be in charge, so Big George just sat in a seat in the front row of the forum and the writers stood bonded together about ten feet away from George. Nobody said anything. The journalists seemed intimidated.

Finally, I asked the first question.

"George, which opponent in your career hit you with the hardest punch?"

The big Foreman grin, which we see now on television, spread across his face from ear to ear.

"Oh boy," he began laughingly. "It happened in the Olympics. A southpaw (left hander) from Europe hit me with a straight left directly on my jaw and I thought he tore my head off. I was able to clinch and get myself together. I made sure to knock him out in the next round. I didn't want to get hit with another one of those punches again. Could he hit!"

The laughter roared out of his mouth and his whole body seemed to enjoy the memory. He was actually jolly.

One of his trainers had been telling me during the last few days how the big heavyweight had been calling his wife every night after his training day was over and he was relaxing in his room.

His pleasant answer to my first question gave me impetus to ask a follow up question. He wasn't such a bad guy after all. Maybe the rumors weren't true.

I followed up remembering the inside information his trainer had given me about the heavyweight calling his wife every night. I thought I'd make him look good and dispel the rumors about how nasty he was. He had been so pleasant answering my first question that this was a natural.

"Is your wife coming to see the fight?" I asked.

"None of your damn business," thundered the seated Mr. Hyde. Dr Jekyll had disappeared and his alternate figure had risen from the ashes. Not only had he risen from the ashes, he had risen from his seat and took two threatening steps towards me, before one of his trainers grabbed him by one arm to stop him.

I almost never get angry, but when someone speaks to me in such a nasty, derogatory tone I blow my cool and want to do battle. I took two steps toward Foreman before one of the other writers grabbed me by the arm and helped save me from suicide.

Foreman then stormed out of the Forum and the so-called press conference was over.

One of the heavyweight's close buddies came over to me and said, "Why did you ask him if his wife was coming to see the fight?"

"I was told he calls her up every night. I was trying to make him look good, because he has a bad reputation."

"They are separated and he's trying to win her back," the buddy told me. "He's very touchy about her, and never mentions her to outsiders."

"But why such an explosion?" I asked.

"That's George," was the answer. "You're lucky you're still alive. He has a mean disposition."

"Amen," Was all I could say.

◆ ◆ ◆

Although this blew over, particularly since Big George knocked out his opponent and I was still alive and walking about in one piece, something truly spectacular happened one year later.

Big George was fighting a Philadelphia fighter, Jimmy Young, in San Juan, Puerto Rico. It was a twelve round fight on a brutally hot night, perhaps one of the hottest nights San Juan had seen in years.

A press conference was held a few days before the fight, sponsored by Don King in a very beautiful restaurant. Naturally I didn't ask any questions of Foreman and made a simple prayer he wouldn't remember our almost go-to the year before. I brought my wife to the conference, as I knew the owner of the restaurant from years gone by.

I did ask Jimmy Young some questions, which he answered gracefully and honestly, but I didn't ask him if his wife was coming to the fight. I don't repeat mistakes.

After the conference my wife and I stopped at the bar downstairs, she for a coke and I for a beer. Don King sidled over and we began a conversation, which ended up in a friendly debate about "fundamental truth."

King's knowledge was amazing, as he quoted everyone from Nietzsche to Kant to Goethe. He was much more than the "clown" we see on television when he hypes one of his productions. He was a man of superior intelligence well beyond his television stand-up bits. When I brought up the philosopher Thomas Aquinas it seemed as though he had read everything Aquinas had written. He was so amazing, that almost everyone at the bar sidled over to listen, and some even joined in the debate. After more than two hours everyone seemed exhausted and one by one retired to their abodes. Even though the restaurant was air-conditioned, the heat seemed to seep through and exhaust what little life everyone had left.

The night of the fight the heat had not abated. It had gotten even worse, and the fans as well as the fighters were sweltering. Air conditioning was of little help as the enthusiasm of the fight crowd always generates excitement, boiling temperaments and lots of betting action.

For twelve rounds Foreman chased Jimmy Young, rarely catching up with him, and the overwhelming belief was that Young should be proclaimed the winner. When the announcer took the slips from the judges his first reading was a draw, meaning the initial judge thought there was no winner, the fight was even, a tie.

Boos came from the rafters, as well as from those having the special ringside seats. Most of the fans felt the Philadelphian had landed enough blows to be awarded the victory. Everyone settled down when the announcer pronounced

Jimmy Young the winner on the next two scorecards, therefore the victor was Young, two votes to zero with one vote a tie. The tie vote was highly suspect.

Foreman, dejected, left the ring with his corner men, one of whom was Gil Clancy, hall of fame trainer and manager. Gil had been training Big George for sometime and knew the heavyweight would be bitter about losing to an opponent who was cleverer than he, but one who could not punch very hard. Gil felt that his fighter would be humiliated, and the aftermath might be disastrous.

They entered the dressing room, nobody saying much of anything. The aura of depression was evident. George stripped and went into the shower. It is best now to tell the rest of this tale in Gil Clancy's words.

"When George finished the shower he came out, his face glowing. There was no bitterness, no anger, only an excited, happy, ecstatic George Foreman. He began screaming, 'I spoke with Jesus. Jesus spoke to me. Jesus blessed me!' He pointed to me and told me Jesus blessed me also, and he blessed my daughter Cathy. Foreman hadn't dressed yet. He was still dripping wet from the shower. Then I saw him looking toward the door leading to the arena where the fans were milling about, some right outside the door hoping to see him when he came out and perhaps get his autograph. I knew what he was thinking. He wanted to tell the world Jesus spoke to him while he was in the shower.

As he started running to the door joyful, happy, glowing, I rammed into him with my shoulder. The other corner man realized what was happening and grabbed him with me. George wanted to spread the word. We didn't want to stop him, but we did want him to put his clothes on before he went back into the arena.

We managed to calm him down, but not his newfound happiness. He was the most joyful human being I have ever seen in my life. And he has remained that way."

The sour reputation the former heavyweight had before the Jimmy Young bout had completely disappeared. Many of you have seen him as a commentator on television fights. The television people rarely use actors who do not present themselves with outwardly joyful dispositions. Actors who can fake joy and happiness perhaps, but not surly sour faced pills, unless the role calls for it.

George has since lived his life as a completely different individual. He has rancor for no one or no thing. He is not an actor in this new life. That smile which reaches from ear to ear is a constant. He loves people, and does his best to preach to others.

We have all noticed how successful he has been with his "Lean Mean Fat Grilling Machine," many of us cook with. What is not generally known is the generosity Foreman has shown in his daily life. How many people know he contributed one million dollars to a hospital in California?

I have been to San Juan, Puerto Rico many times and I am tempted to go into the dressing room in the Forum in which George showered. But I'm afraid. I might turn out to be a nice guy. Then I could interview Big George without trepidation.

Finally, Cathy, Gil Clancy's daughter is the blow-by-blow commentator for Madison Square Garden when New York holds their Golden Gloves each year. Indeed, she is blessed. She does the commentary on the amateur fights with her father, Gil, and she is almost as good as he is.

◆ ◆ ◆

Maria and I returned to New York, to our apartment in the Bronx. Before I relate the next tale I will have to preface it.

Before our marriage, Maria had worked for Grumman and General Cable as an electrical engineer. Her mind was brilliant, and she had the thinking and personality of one who is exceptionally careful, thoughtful, and prudent. Step by step, no short cuts. After our marriage I saw these personality traits in everything she did and the way she did it. I was the wild one, and she the quiet, perceptive part of our duo. I told the jokes and the stories and my dark haired beauty listened, laughed and enjoyed almost everything of a social nature. She never initiated a joke, but responded in a full-throated way to everything that was humorous. In short, she had a great sense of humor, but always let the other person make the wise crack or tell the joke.

One day the telephone rang and she answered it. I was in another room. She called out, "It's for you." As I entered the room where she was standing, holding the phone, I whispered or rather mouthed the words, "Who is it?" Maria put her hand over the speaking part of the telephone and whispered softly, "The Secretary of State."

I knew she was not joking. If she had been it would have been her first joke of our marriage. The expression on her face told me nothing other than it was the Secretary of State. She waited for me to take the phone. I said to her, in hushed tones, "What the Hell does Kissinger want from me?"

"Hello," I said totally befuddled.

The voice on the other end said, "This is Mario Cuomo. I'd like to speak with you about the Boxing Commission in New York. I'm the Secretary of State in New York."

What a relief. I didn't have to answer any war questions from Kissinger. Truthfully, I didn't even know New York had a Secretary of State!

Cuomo is known to be a sports' nut. He played the outfield in the minor leagues before he went into politics, and, as all minor leaguers do, he hoped to make it to the major leagues, but that was not to be. In fact, many people thought he would end up on the Supreme Court.

I eventually made an appointment to meet with Cuomo in his Secretary of State office, which was downtown near City Hall and only three blocks away from Fordham University's School of Education where I received my degree.

Carlos Ortiz, former lightweight champion, and I had become good friends even though my fighter, "Teo" Cruz had won the championship from Carlos. Ortiz would come to my apartment on an occasional Saturday with a six-pack in hand, and we would exchange stories about the past as we imbibed and probably lied a little after the second beer. Maria would busy herself in the kitchen not wanting to interrupt two experts swapping stories about the past.

On one of these Saturdays I told Carlos about Cuomo's call and my intent to meet with him a few short weeks from that day. I told Ortiz that Cuomo had something in mind about boxing, something he wanted to talk about with me and I invited Carlos to join me on my sojourn to the Secretary of State's office on the appointed date.

The former lightweight champ agreed and on the scheduled day I brought him along with me.

Mario Cuomo was delighted to meet Carlos Ortiz and he questioned Ortiz about many of his fights, particularly one in Italy.

Finally, the tall, stately politician made known the purpose of this particular meeting. He told us he wanted to bring the New York State Boxing Commission under his jurisdiction. Presently, James Farley was the head of the commission. His father's cohorts had appointed Commissioner Farley, as the senior Farley was still very dominant in democratic politics.

Cuomo was very impressed with Carlos at the meeting, as the ex-boxer was a very vibrant, knowledgeable individual, particularly when the topic was his favorite subject. He regaled the Secretary with stories about his past career and Cuomo was obviously enthusiastic as he listened with great intensity.

The meeting ended after an hour or so and Mario said he would keep in touch. His own secretary was a young Jewish boy who took notes on everything that was said.

Less than a week later I received a phone call from the young secretary who was an extremely polite and well-informed individual.

"Mr. O'Farrell," he said, "have you heard anything about Carlos Ortiz?"

"No," I truthfully answered.

"We understand there was a problem in which the police were involved."

I knew the champ had not been arrested for anything. If he was partying too hard the police probably let him go.

"I haven't heard a word," I truthfully answered, but my mind visualized Ortiz in all sorts of scrapes. He had a lot of fire in his belly, and was quick to respond to any slight.

Two more phone calls from Cuomo's secretary along the same lines convinced me that Carlos would never become boxing commissioner. As it turned out, Mario Cuomo was not able to wrestle the boxing commission away from Farley.

When Mario became Governor Cuomo of New York State he was able to control the commission and appointed Jose Torres former Lightweight Heavyweight Champion, and friend and mentor to Mike Tyson.

When I first heard New York State now had a Governor Cuomo my mind flashed back to the meeting in the office of the then Secretary of State, and his obvious interest in the boxing exploits of Carlos Ortiz. I also realized that the telephone calls I was receiving from the young secretary to Cuomo about the problems Ortiz was having would probably exclude him from being considered for a high-profile position in the new Governor's Administration. Anything the Republican right could dig up that was adverse to a man who had the potential to be President of the United States in due time was sure to be exploited.

The title "James O'Farrell, Commissioner of Boxing," was music to my ears, even if I made up the tune myself.

With that in mind I telephoned a very dear and close friend of mine, Dr. Edwin A. Campbell. Eddy was the head doctor of boxing for the New York State Boxing Commission, the fellow whose picture you always saw on the Sport's Page of all the New York newspapers "weighing in the fighters," before the fight, to make sure neither fighter came in weighing more than the fight contracts allowed, and also examining them.

We had been friends for years, having dined together and attended functions and award dinners and luncheons as pals.

When he answered the phone in his house his very first words were, "Jimmy, when are we going to get together?"

"Soon, Eddy, but first let me ask you some questions."

"Shoot"

"Does the boxing commissioner have to spend much time in Albany?"

"Some time in Albany and some time in New York."

"You know Cuomo is going to appoint a new Commissioner."

"Oh sure," he answered. "That goes with the territory. Every incoming administration makes changes in many of the departments. Some are pay-offs to constituents and some of the changes go to the most qualified and best man. Cuomo is a good man."

The tune I was humming in my optimistic mind became ever more tuneful.

"Why do you ask, Jimmy?"

"Well, I thought Commissioner O'Farrell sounded pretty good."

Eddie Campbell, ever the dear friend, said to me, "I think you'd make a great commissioner. You were a fighter, a trainer, a manager, a promoter and you know the sport of boxing inside out. Just one question."

"How many constituents would you bring to the table?"

"One," I answered, "me!"

"Make that two," he said. "I think you'd be great. You have the experience and the intelligence."

"So?" I queried.

"Jimmy, two isn't a lot."

"Its more than one," I couldn't resist the wise guy retort. "Twice as many," I joked.

Eddie laughed and asked when we could meet for lunch.

"Anytime," I replied as the tune came to an abrupt ending.

We lunched next week, and I didn't bring up the topic again, although as we left the luncheonette the good doctor called out, "give me a buzz next week and we'll get together again, Commissioner." He smiled a loving smile.

I was neither smiling, singing nor laughing.

"I'll call you, you bum."

◆ ◆ ◆

I never could really see myself as boxing commissioner or commissioner of anything else for that matter. When I was teaching I was offered the job of Assistant Principal or A.P. as it was generally known throughout the school system, but the job of A.P. entails insurmountable paper work, and occasionally helping out a teacher with an unruly student.

It would have been unofficial Assistant Principal until I passed that particular examination, which I knew I could pass. But I had to ask myself the question, "Do I want to be a part of the bureaucratic set-up or do I want to teach students to excel in life, and in the subject I was teaching?"

The answer was easy. I wanted to teach. I always told other teachers in the school if I wanted to become an Assistant Principal or Principal I wouldn't have chosen the school system. I would have chosen a more profitable bureaucracy.

Merrill Lynch hired me the day after I graduated from Fordham University and I worked there the summer before I began teaching. The money was plentiful, triple what I would have made in my first year teaching, but I had no wife and children to support, and my first love was explaining to people something which I knew and might help them later on in life.... students. It wasn't altruism; it was giving myself the pleasure of watching another human being understand that which I was explaining. It was the thrill of seeing the knowing expressions on their faces as the light dawned on what had been perplexed countenances.

I think the beginning of this revelation happened when I was fifteen years old. I was at the beach, Long Beach Long Island, lying in the sand alongside my father soaking up the sun. An older boy, about eighteen years of age, someone I had never met, came up to me and said, "I heard you're a fighter."

I nodded my head and thought to myself, "Do I have to defend myself on a beach day. Is there no end to this fighting?"

He said, "Can you teach me to box?"

What a relief! I don't have to fight an older guy like the one I beat at the Coast Guard at Hoffman Island. I could have kissed this fellow. It was a strange request, but I complied.

"When do you want to learn?" I asked.

"Here and now."

I looked around at the other people sunbathing, and noticed there were only a handful. Almost all of them had their eyes closed and some were actually sleeping.

"Okay," I said getting up and eyeing my very first pupil. He was close to six feet tall, skinny and gangly. I imagine he had been picked on a lot because of his almost emaciated frame.

"Let me see how you hold your hands, in other words the boxing position you use if you have to fight."

It was God-awful. No wonder he came over to a fifteen-year-old kid who knew how to box. He must have taken a handful of beatings from the bullies at school. I didn't have time to feel sorry for him. I had work to do...teaching.

I showed him the correct position to hold his hands. He learned that easily. Then how to maintain his feet so that he could put power into his punches, and finally I told him, "Believe it or not your left jab is your best weapon. Only professional fighters and a few very good amateurs know how to block a left jab.

He followed my instructions to perfection. He snapped his left jab at an imaginary opponent.

"Perfect. Now double it"

"What?"

"Throw two left jabs instead of one."

"Now triple it."

"You mean throw three left jabs, one after the other?"

"Right."

He followed my instruction to perfection.

"When you get home practice what you learned today."

He left with an "Okay" jabbing that imaginary opponent all the way to where his blanket was, some thirty feet from mine. I was ecstatic. He learned everything to perfection, and I was instrumental. I've never had a greater thrill than when I saw the joyful look on his face as he was jabbing his way back to his blanket.

I never saw him again, and I was at the beach every Saturday.

I think God sent him down to deliver a message to me. My inner self got the message, and to this day I've always remembered that eighteen year old and his happiness. I know I was pleased more than he. Had I stayed at Merrill Lynch as they requested, I would probably have an eight-room mansion in a ritzy site, a large bank account, a well-known name in financial circles, but I wouldn't have the picture of so many students whom I will never forget. Thanks God. I got your message and I hope you're happy too, but you owe me one for my ninth-grade nemesis.

◆　◆　◆

There were many students who were interesting and kept you on your toes as their teacher. The most remarkable of these was Geraldine, my Geraldine.

She was a light skinned Negro girl with freckles and red hair. Her face equivocated between dressing in petulance when caught in an egregious act of misbehavior, and a worldwide grin after the necessary bawling out took place. This was always followed by an unabated girlish giggle, which spoke to any realization of guilt as to what she had just done. She was, to put it briefly, a character—devilish, charming, loveable, hateable, but a character.

It was my duty to determine her fate as to graduation into high school, this being my own ninth grade class preparing to enter the upper echelons of schooling.

I had no idea what to do with Geraldine vis-à-vis graduation. Her marks were either failing or slowly crawling toward passing. Her behavior ranged from abominable to loveable, depending on the day, the incidents, the craziness and everything else on the horizon. I came to the conclusion that she should be left back in the ninth grade. It wouldn't be fair to the other students who had studied, worked hard, and behaved in reasonable conformity. I knew I was strict with some, easy with others, but what do you do with a character?

I finally came to the conclusion that my young redhead had to remain in the ninth grade one more year, with the hope that her shenanigans would diminish after learning this lesson. It broke my heart when I thought of her loveable side, but my resolve returned when I remembered all the times she disrupted the class with what seemed to be an innate perversion.

Mr. Chabon was the Assistant Principal in charge of the whole ninth grade and graduation. I searched him out and found him walking the halls of the school in his decisive manner checking for cutters, those who might be cutting class without permission.

He greeted me as I approached him with my face perplexed and my mind torn, but nevertheless determined.

"What's the matter, Jimmy?" he asked. "You look like you're worried."

"Not worried," I answered, "just wrestling with a problem."

"I thought you used to be a fighter. Now you're wrestling?" was his limp attempt at a joke.

"Mr. Chabon, it's Geraldine," I answered.

"You haven't sent her to my office in over a month."

"That's just it. I have sent her there two times this month. Then she comes back to class with some cock-and-bull story about how you told her to behave. She gives me that sweet 'gee I'm sorry grin' and tells me you bawled her out."

"Never happened," Mr. Chabon said. "I haven't seen her this month at all. I have admonished her in the past, but not recently."

"And I believed her. She cons everybody and gets away with it," was my rueful answer. "OK," I continued. "You just made my case. No more doubts. I'm leaving her back. She stays here in the ninth grade one more year and maybe that will shake her up."

Mr. Chabon just stared at me. I could see there was disbelief on his face. "Jimmy think. Think hard."

"What?"

"If we leave her back will you take her in your class next year?" His emphasis was on YOUR.

"No way," my screams almost echoed throughout the halls.

"Now you're thinking," he smiled. "Which teacher do you want her to have if she has to stay? Which teacher?"

"I don't have any enemies," I answered, "and I don't want to start now. Nobody!"

He smiled and said nothing as the light in my dimly lit brain began to dawn.

"Then, what do we do?" I queried.

Mr. Chabon thought for a moment and answered, "We send her on to high school, but she does not attend graduation ceremonies and she does not get a diploma. How's that?"

"Sound like a perfect solution" I replied. "She's not a bank robber, never will be, only a non-conformist, just an adorable nut case," I continued. "Thanks, Mr. Chabon, I can breathe without remorse." I relaxed until the day of graduation.

Geraldine was more than impish on that day; she was unbelievable. Strike that. Nothing the slender five-foot redhead did was unbelievable.

That last day in June was picture perfect; great sun, not too hot, cloudless. The graduation ceremonies were being held in a movie theatre on Southern Boulevard, two blocks away from our school. It was convenient for the parents and children and teachers as well.

The crowd of graduates, with their parents, began to gather half an hour before the doors to the theatre opened. There was a sea of white dresses like beautiful clouds adorning the graduates standing alongside their parents. The dresses were the signs of victory, the signs that these young adults had mastered everything the school had asked them to conquer. The Boulevard was an ocean of happiness and fulfillment.

As I crossed through the traffic to join the groups I couldn't help but be overjoyed watching the happiness which abounded throughout this elongated street in the Bronx, a part of a Boulevard which had seen an ungodly share of crime and debauchery in its recent years.

On my way to greet Mr. Chabon who was in charge of all graduations I stopped cold. Stunned! I was almost hit by a car, and sometimes I wish I had been. There, standing waiting for the theatre doors to open was Geraldine, alongside her diminutive mother. She was wearing the standard white graduation dress! Had Mr. Chabon sabotaged me? The question now was do I approach Geraldine, or do I search out our Assistant Principal for an explanation. The deal was no diploma, no graduation ceremony and the imp goes on to high school. What about the mother standing alongside my little redhead? Do I upset her unnecessarily? No. Chabon first. There he is standing at the far corner of the theatre.

I ran over to him. "Irving," I said as I dispensed with the formal Mr. Chabon. "What the Hell is going on here?"

He looked at me enigmatically as if I were bereft of my senses.

"Jimmy, are you all right?"

"I'm fine, at least I was fine until seconds ago." I took him by the arm, moved him to the center of the crowd where he could get a first hand look. He exploded. "Geraldine!"

"Correct"

"And she's wearing a white graduation dress!"

"Did you undermine me?" I questioned.

Mr. Chabon sputtered, looked at me, looked back at the mother and her child as the doors to the theatre opened, just as my misfit entered with the surge of the crowd.

"Jimmy, I swear to God." I didn't let him finish. "You swear to God what?"

"I had her brought to my office and told her, no graduation ceremony, no diploma."

He thought for a moment and began asking me, "You don't think...?"

"Of course," I replied. "That's the only answer. She told her mother she was graduating along with the rest of her class and the other ninth graders, and got her mother to buy her a white graduation dress. Momma doesn't know, and she may never know!"

Mr. Chabon was stunned. "But she will have to go up on the stage with her class and receive a diploma. That means there will be one diploma short. I arranged for thirty-three diplomas and there are thirty-four students in her class. Knock her out and there are thirty-three diplomas and thirty-three graduates."

I was calmed down by this time, everything sinking in gradually. "Irving, somehow she will work it out. She has more inventions than Thomas Edison."

The ceremonies went off gracefully, each class entering the stage, and each student being handed a diploma by the principal of the school, Mrs. Conroy. The crowd stood and applauded, cheering loudly throughout the whole ceremony. After the events were finished, special awards handed out; the crowd began the evacuation from the theatre.

I went to the lobby as graduates passed by and crowded outside the theatre. Parents and siblings greeted their own special graduate and mingled directly outside. I was waiting to spot Geraldine. I saw her mother and stood an appreciable distance away. Geraldine had to get to her mother. Finally I saw her run to Momma, and I managed to squirm close enough to the two of them so that I could hear the ensuing conversation.

"I didn't see you up there Gerry," the mother said.

"Momma, I was standing next to that tall girl Valerie. She always blocks everyone out of the way, cause she wants to be a star."

"And where's your diploma?' the mother inquired.

"I asked Wilma to hold it for me. I told her you were gonna take me out to lunch so I didn't want to take a chance on loosing it. She'll give it to me when I see her again. I told her my mommy was taking me out to a special lunch and I didn't want to take a chance of loosing it. Come on Mommy," she said as she squeezed her mother's arm wheeling her through the crowd. As she passed me she called out, "Hi Mr. O'Farrell" that broad grin on her face.

"Congratulations," I yelled back to a girl who had probably spent the whole two hours in the ladies room, dreaming of other adventures and congratulating herself on how she beat the system. When I called out "Congratulations" to Geraldine in the lobby I was sincere. No one else I know has the initiative that ninth-grader had. My only hope is she has put this uncanny initiative to good use. Somehow I have a feeling she has. Years later I still think about her. She was and always will be "My Geraldine."

◆   ◆   ◆

Dan Klores may very well be the premier Public Relations agent in the United States, arguably in the world. Jennifer Lopez is among the personalities whom he represents as of this writing (so many things change in the P.R, field).

Dan is a quiet, comforting man in his forties who not only knows his trade of garnering publicity for his clients, but also has gone beyond his trade and become a documentary producer. A few years ago he produced a simple, but exquisite, documentary about the boys with whom he had grown up in Brooklyn. He captured them as they were today with a brilliance that won him great acclaim at the Cannes Film Festival, a yearly event known worldwide.

I did not know Dan personally, but I heard he was making another documentary about Emile Griffith, former Welterweight Champion. I realized I knew more about Emile other than his family and his two managers.

I called Klores at his home, left a message and waited for this return call. Within days I received the return call, explained my association throughout the years with the champ and told the producer he could use me in the documentary if he wished.

He was pleased with my call and made arrangements with me to be filmed at an outdoor place overlooking a lake, three days later.

◆   ◆   ◆

I took a ribbing from my wife's family about how nervous I would be and how I would foul up the whole documentary. The night before my to-be appearance my brother-in-law, Peter Lopez, kidded me.

"You'll probably stutter so much they'll probably throw the whole thing out the window."

"I'm an experienced veteran of film," I half kidded back.

"Tell me about all your starring film experience," he challenged a humongous grin on his Puerto Rican face.

"Didn't you know I was on Merv Griffin's television show, twice," I grinned back.

"I never saw you. When was this?"

"Before I married your sister-in-law, Maria"

"How did this happen?"

"I went down with Anne, my first wife; we were interviewed, accepted and appeared on the show as contestants. We won."

"What did you win?"

"A sewing machine, but Anne didn't sew, so we sold it."

"What was the name of the show, and how did it work?"

"Play your Hunch was the name of the show, and here's how it worked. We competed against another couple. Merv Griffin brought out three characters, one of which was…let's say an upcoming actress who was not known yet. Now you have A, B and C standing in front of the competing couples. We had to write down on a piece of paper, which one was the true upcoming actress. The other two were phonies of course."

"I picked out the correct one, so we won."

My brother-in-law thought for a moment.

"You said you were on the show twice." A grin enveloped his face indicating he thought he had caught me in a lily-white fib.

◆   ◆   ◆

"I was. It was almost a year later. Gil Clancy and I had been to fights in lower Manhattan and we decided to top the night with a couple of drinks at the Page Two, a cocktail lounge on the East side at 34th Street.

It was rather late and there were only two other fellows seated together in deep conversation. Finally one of them called to us and said, "Do you guys know any professional fighters?" Gil and I cracked up. Serendipity was at work full throttle.

"You mean like the ones you see on television? The ones who are punching at each other?" I asked with my innocent baby face look, the gee-wiz look I always used when I was putting someone on.

"Exactly," the poor innocent replied with enthusiasm.

"Pete, Clancy had to restrain himself from choking as he watched this routine take place."

The fellow at the other end of the bar came over to us and introduced himself, hoping we knew someone in boxing that he could use on his show, someone who had been or was then involved in boxing. He gave us his name, told us he was now producing Play Your Hunch and shook our hands hopefully.

"This is Gil Clancy," I told him.

"And this is Jimmy O'Farrell," Gil said.

The young producer smiled and continued with his question. "Well, do you know anybody in boxing?"

I motioned to Gil and told this uninformed sports follower, "Gil has managed and trained three champions. Boxing champions."

Clancy chimed in and said, "Jimmy was a fighter for eight years and he's training and managing fighters now."

The producer looked at us in a sizing-over manner and didn't know quite what to make of this whole thing. Clancy had a movie-star face, square chin, black curly hair, and I looked like an altar boy who had never sinned in his life.

Peter broke into my story. "Never sinned in his life, hah!"

"Peter," I said, "let me finish the story."

"I called the bartender over and said to him, 'Normy, who is this?'" pointing to my handsome buddy. Normy had known us for many years.

"Why, what's up?" he asked.

"Just tell this fellow standing here who this is."

Normy started walking away without answering.

"Come back, Norm," I yelled. He did.

"I'm serious. This fellow standing with us now is looking for information. He's a television producer, so this is important." Norman filled the producer in on Gil's background and our newfound friend seemed satisfied.

Then Gil asked our bartender to identify me. Normy did, and the producer called to the friend he had been drinking with to come over and join us.

He told his buddy about us and said, "Which one, do you think?"

Clancy said, "Not me," so I was chosen. Pete interrupted again, "so what happened?"

"The two of them were now enthusiastic. I assumed the second fellow was a co-producer or something because he gave me the studio's address and the time I should be there. He gave me a telephone number and asked me to call him the morning before the show was to go on air. I guess he wanted to be sure I was still alive. I never mentioned I had been on the show the year before."

My brother-in-law asked, "How did you know they weren't putting you on?"

"They would have had to have been the best actors this side of Broadway," I answered him. Pete was always looking for something out of whack.

"In fact when I was on the first Play Your Hunch I put on Merv Griffin!"

"The show where you won the sewing machine?"

"Yeah, here's what happened. You know how the host of these game shows always introduces the contestants, asking them where they're from, what they do, blah, blah, blah."

"Yeah"

"Well when Griffin came to me he asked me what I did."

"Yeah?"

"He said, "Mr. O'Farrell what do you do?" Instead of answering I looked at him blankly. My wife kicked me under the table, with an answer him stupid kick. I knew the show was live; they weren't taping, so I wanted my timing to be exact.

Griffin got the shakes. He thought I froze. I could see it on his face. He recovered a bit when I repeated his question slowly, as if I wasn't sure what he meant, so he expanded his question as if he were talking to a moron.

"Yes," he said, "What do you do for a living?"

"I had him in my trap." He had that come on will you we haven't got all day look on his face and in his voice.

"I'm a school teacher, But You Want To Know What I Do For A Living!!" I answered. At that time schoolteachers were being paid miserly salaries, not like today.

The audience got it right away and roared and applauded. Griffin's face turned red and he stammered something, which gave me time to plug my beauty parlor, something that's a no-no.

"I own the Castro and O'Farrell beauty parlor" I finished up.

"You really trapped Merv Griffin? Lopez queried. "You're not putting me on?"

"God's honest truth," I replied.

"So then what happened the day of the show?"

"Well, the format had changed slightly from the year before. The two husbands and wives were still on stage right,"

"Stage what?"

"Forget it. The right side of the stage, OK"

"OK"

"And the three possibilities, in this case former fighters, were now center stage facing the audience.

"Center stage I can understand, I'm getting an education."

"Shut up."

"Go on I want to know what happened!"

"Before the three of us came out I had to stand behind a screen punching a speed bag for a few seconds. The contestants and the audience could see my silhouette, but vaguely. The rat-tat-tat of the punching bag garnered both their audio and visual attention. A silhouette only gives away the general size and the outline of the individual.

The producer had lined up a gruff looking fellow my size and shape to be possibility 'A', and I had talked them into using Jack Gelber, a friend of mine, as possibility 'B'. Jack was a playwright who had won an OBIE and written a Broadway play."

"What's an OBIE?"

"Shut up"

"I won't listen anymore till you tell me what an OBIE is."

"OK, an OBIE is what is says it is. An award is given to the best actor, playwright, etc for plays that are not on Broadway, plays that are off Broadway, ergo, OB equals Off Broadway."

"What about the IE in OBIE."

"How the Hell do I know."

"What about ergo?"

"What do you mean?"

"You just said it. You said ergo OB equals Off Broadway."

"Will you let me finish if I tell you what ergo means?"

Peter Lopez grinned and we both knew he was breaking my chops and asking legitimate questions at the same time.

"Ergo is Latin for therefore, and I know this because I flunked Latin twice."

"You really flunked it twice?"

"Yup, so that makes me some kind of expert. Anyhow I like to use ergo because it's simpler than therefore and it sounds classier. I taught 'ergo' to my two kids, that's why they're so classy."

"I never heard them use it."

"You've only seen them twice."

"That's no excuse."

"Next time you see Anne Marie or Jimmy I'll have them use two words."

"Which are?"

"Up yours."

Lopez laughed so hard he rolled off the couch holding his rotund belly. Finally, when he finished laughing, he got back on the couch and said, "Now that's a classy family. Tell me what happened at Play Your Hunch. You didn't finish."

"Of course I didn't finish. You keep interrupting."

"I won't interrupt no more."

"Anymore, not no more."

"Finish, finish." I knew Pete didn't like my correcting his English. It was always my way of getting back at him and he knew it. But he knew I loved him.

"Anyhow, after I finished punching the speed bag Griffin told the audience and the contestants a professional fighter had been doing the punching and they would now enter. The three of us came out from behind the curtain and walked to center stage. I was breathing heavily as I hadn't punched a bag in some time. Jack Gelber noticed my breathing and managed to simulate someone who had been exercising by taking quick, short breaths.

Now we had 'A', 'B' and 'C' facing a live television audience 'A' a short gruff well built tough looking…well I won't say beast, but you wouldn't want to meet him in a dark alley. 'B' Jack Gelber, breathing like a steamboat in a hurry, and yours truly 'C' trying to breathe like a corpse.

The first contestants were asked which one had been a professional fighter?"

"You" said Pete Lopez.

"One more crack like that and you won't hear the end of the story."

"OK, I promise"

"Obviously the first contestants chose 'A'. Turned out 'A' was an accountant working for a prestigious bank in mid-town Manhattan. He was highly intelligent and from our conversations before the show a very sweet guy. If you ran into him in an alley he'd probably lend you money.

Now the husband and wife contestants remaining had to choose between Gelber, 'B', and me 'C'. The married couple talked it over for what seemed like centuries. If they were wrong they'd be finished and unable to come back the next day and face a new couple.

Finally, and remember, there was money riding on this."

"What do you mean, people were betting?" Pete asked.

"No, the program was going to pay one hundred and fifty dollars each to "A," "B" & "C," that's the accountant, Jack Gelber and me, if neither of the contestants guessed right. If one of the two pairs guessed right we would receive one hundred dollars each. So we all tensed up, rooting for a wrong guess and one hundred and fifty bucks instead of the hundred."

"So?" the veteran numbers and horseplayer asked, "Who did they pick as the professional fighter?"

"Who do you think?" I teased.

"Do I get any prize if I guess right?" Pete teased back.

"You'll get a punch in the mouth, if you don't tell me who the contestants picked," I answered.

"O.K., they picked you"

"Why do you say they picked me?" I queried.

"Because you were the professional fighter," he answered.

"Peter, are you putting me on? They don't know who the fighter is. Am I conversing here with a Dum-Dum?" Lopez laughed out loud. "I never watch quiz shows. Just horse racing on T.V.G."

"That's why you're always broke," I laughed.

"Let's see," he broke in. "They have to choose you or your buddy, as the fighter. All right, they picked your buddy, and you all made the hundred and fifty bucks each because they were all wrong."

"What made you say that?" I asked.

"Because you wouldn't be telling me the story if you didn't collect the one fifty."

"You're right," I said, "but I'm telling you my television appearances in reference to tomorrow's T.V. documentary."

"You talked so long about your conquests on television I forgot you're doing a documentary tomorrow. You ought to be a storyteller. Anyhow, you'll screw-up tomorrow."

"Why?"

"You'll find a way. I know you. You always find a way to screw-up."

"And I always called you my favorite brother-in-law." I countered.

"You still do, and still will," he came back.

"Why?"

"Because we're both degenerate horse players. One degenerate can always spot another. It's a brotherhood. Even a brother-in-law hood."

"You know, I'll never forget my first appearance when I was a contestant with my wife against another couple, my debut, so to speak."

"What happened?" Peter asked.

"When we won, the audience began clapping the way they always do when there's a winner. I heard the audience applaud and began clapping with them without thinking. The producer of that show ran over to me as the camera panned the people seated in the auditorium. His face was consumed with anger."

"Stop clapping for yourself, stop clapping for yourself," he literally screamed at me, and then ran away before the camera came back.

"I was humiliated. I thought I looked so stupid. That haunts me even to this day."

"Winners always carry on when they win in these contest shows. The producers always tell them to jazz it up," Peter said.

"I thought you didn't watch contest show," I said.

"I saw Wheel of Fortune once," he said. "They carry on like someone goosed them."

"Are you trying to make me feel better?" I asked.

"No," he answered, "cause I know you're gonna screw up tomorrow."

"Let me look at the racing form," I told him trying to change the subject.

"If there's a horse named 'screw-up' I'll bet on him" he finished our usual bizarre conversation.

◆ ◆ ◆

Tomorrow came. Dan Klores had arranged to have a limousine pick me up at eleven in the morning. Five minutes before the car was due the telephone rang. I was halfway out the door dressed in my first class clothes, which was a far cry from Beau Brummel, although nowadays that doesn't seem to matter much.

After picking up the phone I heard a soft, young voice with an obvious Southern drawl ask if this was the O'Farrell residence. My acknowledgement assured the soft voice that "Yes, this was Jim O'Farrell."

"I'm lost," the young voice said. "Can you tell me how to get to your house? I'm supposed to pick you up."

"Where are you now," I asked.

"I don't know," was the answer.

The Pete Lopez curse was kicking in. I knew Klores's crew was waiting for me, but this initial screw-up was not of my making. I got some information out of the limo driver as to what his surroundings look like, although I had the initial thought that my part in this documentary about Emile Griffith might be on life support before I left my house.

I managed to get a feel for where he was, and it appeared he was ten minutes or so away. He followed my instructions and arrived within the next twenty minutes. When I entered the limo the driver asked, "Where to?" Now I began cursing Pete Lopez, albeit I had not personally done anything negative at this point.

"To the shoot," I answered.

"Where is that?" he asked.

"Didn't Mr. Klores tell you?" I asked.

"He just told me to pick you up at this address," was his reply. He didn't say nuthin else sir," was the bewildered answered. I was tempted to direct him to Pete Lopez's house and help me get rid of my Jonah, but Klores was waiting for me and time was becoming essential.

"Get on your cell phone and call him up," I asserted.

"Didn't bring no cell phone."

I knew I had to think fast. It was eleven thirtyish and a camera crew cost money. I was sure Klores was working on a tight budget in spite of his success with his first documentary. Awards certainly help the profit margin, but overspending cuts in to the financial take and I didn't want to screw-up (there's that word again) and cause added costs to what I thought might be a problematic moneymaker.

"O.K. lets start from the beginning. Where were you when you last saw Mr. Klores or one of his staff?"

"Up in a building by a lake," was the answer.

"Was Mr. Klores actually standing at the building?" I asked.

"Yes sir,"

"Then let's go back to that building" I said as my face flushed and my heart fluttered in anticipation."

"Not sure how," was the enigmatic answer.

"Just re-trace your steps," I offered.

"O.K." The limo took off with the driver constantly looking at a map. I envisioned a nice ride to nowhere. After a half hour drive we arrived close to a lake.

"Could be that building across from the lake," I said as I pointed to what appeared to be a municipal building.

"No, but I think we're close," the driver said as we both saw there was no one in sight. I mean no one. It was a Saturday and not a soul was in view.

"Maybe it's at the other end," the young boy said as he quickly turned the car around and headed back in the direction from which we had just come. After fifteen or so blocks he said, "That's the building." Something had dawned on him. I looked around and saw a movie theatre and a few shopping stores.

"Which one, I don't see any building?" I asked.

"The one back there…where we were."

"Turn the car around," I ordered, "and we'll see what's there." He sped back and stopped in front of the municipal building he had first thought might be the correct locale.

I got out and found the door to the building unlocked. I walked into an empty hallway with offices on both sides. I was reasonably frantic by this time. I walked down the hallway turning the knobs to every office, fearing I might walk into the middle of a Mafia meeting or a simple divorce case as each office had the name of a lawyer or a legal entity emblazoned on the glass part of the door. Each door was locked which meant I couldn't even ask if anyone had seen a camera crew on or near the premises. This first floor had about ten legal offices, none of which was unlocked. Golf Saturday I thought to myself. Perhaps Sailing Saturday would be more appropriate.

There was a staircase leading to the second floor. Why not try it. Bingo, a door at the end of this hall opened and a room filled with men and a camera.

One man stepped forward and asked, "Jim O'Farrell?"

"Dan Klores?" I queried. We shook hands and he said, "We're running late, lets go down by the lake."

Everyone followed Dan and me as we worked our way to the edge of the waters, which were surrounded by benches.

"Any trouble getting here?" was Dan's question to me.

"Not really," I answered. "We just took a tour of Canada on our way."

The producer laughed and began telling me how they had just "shot" members of the commission in the commission's office in this building and how they seemed hopelessly inept and uninformed about boxing. He had interviewed dozens of fighters, managers and others associated with the sport.

This was not particularly good news for me as I was sure it would not be longer than a two hour documentary and judging from the list of names he reeled off it seemed as though he already had enough material for a day long drama.

"We're going to shoot you sitting on a bench overlooking the lake," he told me. "One thing I'd like you to do is repeat the question I asked you, then answer."

We reached the bench he had chosen and a member of the crew miked me, microphone unseen. His questions began, "How did you get into boxing?" I answered his question. He asked a second question. I answered it. Then it hit me. I had forgotten to repeat the questions as Dan had instructed me. Two goofs. Two unnecessary goofs. Two Pete Lopez screw-up goofs.

In my own planning ahead of time I had remembered JFK's method of using his right hand in a chopping manner when he wanted to emphasize an important point vehemently. By this time with all that had happened I was so flummoxed that I found myself right hand chopping when I was asked a simple question such as "What date did your fighter 'Teo Cruz' become champion?" It looked like I was angry, or arguing, or Lord knows what, over a simple factual answer. Then things got worse. This genial producer cut the camera, and as it stopped rolling came over and sat next to me on the bench.

"Jim," he purred, "do you know what you just said?"

"Sure, I was saying Ray Robinson was and will be the greatest fighter of all time." Klores finished it for me, "and you said he was the Michael Jackson of boxing."

"Right," I continued, "he was the Michael Ja…. what, I said Michael JACK-SON?" I was in the throes of the Lopez curse. "I meant" "Jordan, Michael Jordan," he finished.

"Do you want me to leave now?" I asked.

Dan laughed a kindly laugh and told me no, they would edit it and have a re-do, re-do a word that always meant do it over, even when I was playing stickball as a kid in a schoolyard. We did it over; I got it right and began counting the cost of the editing and re-doing in my simplistic mind. "Will I ever do anything right?' I asked myself. At least the limo driver could plead youthfulness and unfamiliarity with the territory. Acting and speaking was my territory. I'm sure the young boy didn't have a brother-in-law who put the hex on him was my only excuse to myself.

The shoot finished shortly thereafter and the limo took me home without a hitch. Needless to say I was not in the documentary, but my name did appear in the credits right above Carlos Ortiz who also did not make the final cut. I beat Carlos again, but only because O'Farrell precedes Ortiz alphabetically. Blessings for scintillas of favors.

◆　◆　◆

When schoolteachers retire they rejoice in the release of the monumental burdens they have been carrying throughout the many years. This austerity associated with classroom teachers dissolves like a melting ice floe in the arctic summer. The beginning of retirement holds promise of freedom to fulfill the many pleasures they had dreamed of the major part of their lives. Tennis, travel, golf, and perhaps a little tutoring on the side to pick up some extra money, which will help supplement the retirement pay.

Joe Demas simply followed the path he had been traveling as he was teaching, racehorse betting. Only now, with retirement, he has expanded. Lest you think I speak of betting in a pejorative manner, allow me to disabuse you. Handicapping horse races is an art form of mathematics. A lower form of math I agree, but how many of us use algebra as we are sent out to pasture after X number of schooling.

Joe comes from an Italian family of five, one of whom was a high-ranking police officer, his dad. No, Poppa didn't arrest son Joe for betting on horses, because betting on horses became legal when our governing bodies realized they could get a piece of the action by opening OTB offices. The initials OTB stand for Off Track Betting. Their coffers prospered when they could add to their profligate budgets.

The insane idea that betting inside a racetrack was legal, but betting a horse as you stand one step outside of the track was breaking the law dawned on our politicians as a hypocritical plague on their electorate; therefore, OTB offices sprang up all over the country.

Mr. Demas was a Social Studies teacher in a New York City high school, until, as he said, "I was tired of listening to my own voice." To relieve this pain, he would often make visits to the aforementioned OTB sanctuaries, usually after consulting with the Math teacher in his high school. Turned out the Math teacher was uninformed as to the relationship between charting horses, which would win races, and the simple Math with which he was inundating his students. To put it simply, this mathematician never gave our hero, Mr. Demas, any winners.

Joe decided he would strike out on his own as he ventured to clear his mind on the various lunch trips. His mind, not his wallet. Patrons of OTB saw this blondish, lithe, egregiously energetic figure with the good looks change from a loser to a winner.

He also changed from a Social Studies teacher to a Guidance Counselor, knowing well the evils of sinful behavior. All the students he counseled looked up to Mr. Demas. His intelligence and feel for people endeared him to many. He no longer "had to listen to my own voice." Rather, he listened to the voices of those who came to him for advice or those who were choosing the fork in the road which led to disaster, or less than happy lives.

One of his triumphs was the now renowned author James McSherry. The McSherry family consisted of five siblings including James. Joe had counseled two of this Irish clan before he came across James. The first two were frustrating to Mr. Demas. When James came into his office, Joe picked up a book and whacked him across the head. James was bewildered.

"You're the third McSherry I've counseled and, unlike the others, you're going to make it," Joe blazed. He had long counseling sessions with the author-to-be, kept in touch with him after he graduated and continued on to Columbia Universities' Writing Program.

Mr. Demas, a bachelor, often let James use his apartment to do much of his writing. "Bronx Astronomy" a collection of short stories, and "Crime Scene Reporter," an autobiographical one-man show were the results.

The latest by McSherry, a book entitled "A Clean Street's a Happy Street," has met with great acclaim. I had the good fortune to read the book and it knocked me out.

Joe Demas, in the meantime, followed the tune his own piper played for him. The injection of success with James and other students he counseled were re-invigorating experiences and he harkened back to his first love, horses.

He, with close friends, bought a few trotting horses. Initially they had their share of winners, a good time, lots of fun, but eventually empty pockets. Joe found it exciting watching his horses finish first past the finish line. After a while, the horses forgot where the finish line was, and Joe and his crew decided not to send out the search parties. The conclusion of this venture was that harness racing was not worthwhile. It had to be thoroughbred racehorses, not trotters.

After his retirement from the public school system in New York, the energetic retiree gathered a few of his buddies and began claiming thoroughbred horses that raced at Belmont and Aqueduct racetracks in New York.

A claiming race is a race in which the owner enters his horse with the knowledge that any other owner can claim (literally buy) the horse before the race begins, and consequently own the horse after the race is over. If the horse breaks his leg during the race, well, tough luck Kidoo to the unfortunate individual who claimed the horse before the race began.

These "claiming" races in New York range in price from ten thousand dollars to ninety thousand dollars, depending on the owner's belief in the quality of his horse.

◆ ◆ ◆

I was fortunate enough to encounter Joe at Yonkers raceway, a trotting palace at night, and a simulcast center during the day. Races from all over the country were simulcast for viewing from one o'clock until the last race had ended.

I noticed this fellow running around, buying coffee and eats for his friends who were seated together in a joy of camaraderie watching the races and betting independently or together at the betting window.

I somehow managed to join the group and seated myself in an inconspicuous manner. Four of them were retired schoolteachers and I made the fifth. It crossed my mind that we would have appeared so out of character if our former students could see us as we screamed and cursed the horses we bet on when they proved to be late to the finish line. Laggards are losers we frequently taught our former students, and the pigs we cursed proved it. Not very genteel I must admit.

The least of the losers was Demas. He had a quick mind and a solid handicapping style. So much so that when I found out he was also involved in claiming horses with other people, I wanted in. I was really interested. The people, his unofficial partners, consisted of two ladies (one a retired school principal), a retired Chief Operating Officer of an insurance company, a full time lawyer, Joe's brother, the father of Joe's horse trainer, and Joe himself.

I watched their operation and saw that this impressive ex-guidance counselor was the unofficial manager of a group that had a shot at making a profit as well as enjoying themselves in fantasyland. After all, doesn't everybody dream of owning a Kentucky Derby horse? Don't people line the rafters and actually go out of state to win the million dollar lotteries? Remember the song from the Broadway show "South Pacific," "If you don't have a dream, how you gonna make a dream come true?"

Realizing choosing horses is an imprecise science I decided that for five thousand dollars I could become part of this no name horse owner grouping, so I joined.

Not only was Demas himself beating the horses, but he also took on the IRS. Joe worked every day including Saturday and Sunday, keeping records of his winnings, losses, and expenses. The year he had a loss for the twelve months, he included it in his tax return form. They challenged him and he convinced them it was his business. He made every losing ticket available to the government, a complete and accurate list of his winners, and everything else they demanded. The government conceded he was a businessman devoting full time to his own private business. The kicker was he didn't pad a thing. He was totally honest. This was typical Joe Demas, unlike other businessmen who often make their figures do the walking.

As I became a part of our horse-owners group I enjoyed watching our first horse Bricks. We claimed this beauty for thirty thousand dollars and, when we put him in his next race, his original owner claimed him back from us for thirty five thousand dollars; a five thousand profit minus food and training expenses.

Our second claimer was Catlike Move. He really lived up to his name. As I stood at the finish line, our "Cat" came storming down the stretch of the race-track taking dead aim at the leader. He came to the leader, fought him head to head, nose to nose right to the finish line. It looked like a dead heat, wherein both horses cross the finish line at exactly the same time, but the stewards who deter-mined the winner put up a picture showing our "Cat" less than a nose in back of his rival. Our baby was second.

There is nothing so thrilling as standing at the finish line watching your horse fighting his heart out trying to pass the leader. It was love at first sight; a memory you will never forget. That horse became your child and you wanted to take him home with you, your wife not withstanding. My wife understood when I revealed what happened, but of course I left the horse with our trainer Dominick Galluscio. He wouldn't fit in our apartment. Dominick would, but the horse wouldn't.

We received twenty percent of the purse, which amounted to six thousand dollars, and as we were leaving the track at the end of the day, I told Steve Tobin, our partner and retired CFO, "The Cat will win next time out."

Catlike Move won this next race and we were up over fifty thousand dollars.

My hero, Joe Demas, decided we should claim other horses with the money we now had. Joe must have been communing with the Math teachers at his for-mer school. The "Cat" had finally been claimed from us for a good price and we were flush with money. Joe studied the Racing Form with unusual vigor and unusual pathos. As the cliché tells us he lost his touch. We paid thirty five thou-sand for a horse who loved to run to the first turn of the racetrack. After reaching that turn in second or third place he decided to give the others a chance and retreated faster than some of President Lincoln's generals during the Civil War. We thought he might have a breathing problem; consequently, we had a vet oper-ate on wherever the Hell he breathed. That was no help. He still retreated after the first turn. We tried gelding him. When horses, male horses, are unusually attracted to female horses they are often dissuaded from this inclination by a horse surgeon leaving him an equine eunuch. This did nothing to stop his retreats. The cost of the operations and the cost of his upkeep made our nest egg look like Houdini had come back to initiate a disappearing act.

Joe decided to send the horse to another racetrack in another state. At this writ-ing the horse has run twice, won twice, and searches for turns in this track, Charles Town, as he whispers to the other horses, "Try and catch me." They don't.

Demas, arguably the nicest fellow you will ever meet, has redeemed himself, and all is well with our conglomerate of retirees.

Epilogue

An Open Letter to My Son

Dear Jim,

Don't blame me for my lengthy stories about myself. You told me to let it all hang out and you pretty much got what you asked for.

When I was a young boy I often wondered this or that about my father, but in those times you didn't dare to ask him to go into any details. You didn't ask anything. All the tidbits of information concerning my Pop were learned from the crumbs of sentences he would occasionally drop, and you would have to imagine the rest.

Not that he had any deep dark secrets, just that it was not your place, as a son, to be asking questions. Any information re: his life he kept to himself, other than to lecture and use something in his life as an example.

I think you and I have been close throughout our relationship, as your sister, Anne Marie, and I have. What you don't know is insignificant and really not worth telling, or talking about.

The day I told you I would give you some extra money if your marks improved you said, "You trying to bribe me?" I didn't answer because I didn't have an answer. I have an answer now. "No son, I want to reward you." Maybe that will get me off the hook, because here you are now writing books and asking my advice about this and that.

I think this makes me a pretty good Dad. I know the love I have for you surpasses any deficiencies I may have shown throughout the years. You and Anne Marie are the loves of my life, even more so than the racehorses I wanted to bring home.

Good luck with the rest of this book. The next one we talked about writing sounds fascinating. Please permit me to write an introduction. I'll keep it to one page.

A Son's Tale (Me)

I know I have a father. My sister told me so, and she knows all those kind of things.

My mother and this man yelled at each other a lot. I never thought anyone won the yelling matches, but I was just a kid who had graduated from the cradle to crawling on the floor. I hadn't reached the status of referee.

When I was able to eat at the dinner table, my mom, sister and I ate watching television. Not the programs I would like, but what the heck. The food was good and I was up with the big guys.

When I began to walk steadily I often heard my sister call this man Dad or Daddy, so I called him Daddy too. It felt good.

This fellow often played with me when he was in the house, and I got to like him a lot whenever I saw him, which wasn't often. When I played in the backyard with other kids they would occasionally use the word Daddy, which meant they had one too. Often, when he was home, he would use the phrase "this family." That meant us.

So what my sister told me was true. This towering figure was my Dad. As I got older the towering figure shrunk. Either that or I got taller. My sister told me I was growing up, which, I guess, meant he was growing down.

The day I had to start school he took me by the hand to the school. I fought him like a tiger, but he won as usual. I ended up in a schoolyard on a line with lots of other kids. It wasn't bad. It was terrible. Some months later they tell me I had an accident. I tried to knock a truck over, but it was moving pretty fast. I guess I lost because I ended up in a hospital.

My dad had taken me to a gymnasium before my fight with the truck and I met Emile Griffith World Welterweight Champion. He came to the hospital and helped me get well. They took out my spleen, so I got better.

It was all becoming clear after I got out and had to go back to that school. I would really have liked to go back and fight the truck. I think I would have won the second time, because Dad was always bringing professional fighters to the house and they were showing me things abut fighting. Now, this was learning. The heck with school was my thought. School was a house of horrors.

♦   ♦   ♦

From the conversations I head in the house I came to realize my mother and father were both teacher. Ugh! Also Dad taught school at night. They called it adult education. What idiots went there? Daddy must have loved punishment too. When he went to the gym in the afternoons he taught his fighters what he had learned as a fighter. More teaching. I was able to figure out that he had been a fighter because there were pictures of him knocking out fighters all over the house. I think he hid the pictures of other guys knocking him out.

When I was thirteen we moved from our Garden apartment in the Bronx to a complex call Le Havre in Whitestone, Long Island. The high school there wasn't so bad, because Dad knew Dave Lerner a Social Study teacher in the school.

Mr. Lerner and Dad had previously taught at night school together and were close friends. At that time Dave drove a beat up green Buick with no rear-view mirror.

With Dave as my Social Study teacher, and a close friend with all my other teachers I knew I had to shape up. If not, there would be a telephone call to my house in teacher's code relaying a message, the point of which would be that your son is goofing off, and you had better do something about it. The long arm of O'Farrell reached across to Bayside High School.

If the telephone rang and I head Mr. Lerner was on the line I wouldn't have to tap the line or learn the code to translate the conversation. Net result, I hit the books.

Soon, learning became fun. It was like a game. A game called "Beat the teachers." And my pop never had to lay a hand on my bottom. Come to think of it, he never, ever laid a hand on me when I was younger. I think I know the reason. I was the fifth wall in every room. Nobody ever knew I was in the house until I tackled that truck. I graduated from Bayside High School, not with honors, but with relief.

Mr. Lerner wised up and started his own business selling very secure financial instruments. He started his own business and called it "David Lerner & Associates," which he has had until this day. You may have heard his radio commercials. I guess he's a big shot. The one thing I remember when Dad was teaching night school was his coming home and saying, "I think Dave Lerner is the best teacher in the city. He mesmerizes his students, and they responded." As an aside he would try to sell them stocks and bonds, as night school was for adults, and he made them interested.

Dad admired Mr. Lerner as much as he admired anyone. Dave had polio, limped badly, but never let it deter him from his goals. Dad knew that through their friendship and Mr. Lerner's incessant goal driven energy I would succeed in high school. I have to take some credit. I showed up every day.

◆　◆　◆

After only a year or so in Whitestone I became the fourth wall. Dad left the house without any notice. Mom was upset and tried not to show it, but the little attention I had received previously became negligible. My sister, Anne Marie, kept saying, "He will come back," but he didn't. He got his own apartment back in the Bronx and made arrangements to see my sister and me on weekends. It wasn't the same. Maybe I missed the arguments, because they had become a staple of our every day living, but that dreaded word divorce crept in.

After they allowed me to graduate from Bayside High school, I enlisted in Queensboro College and Bingo I graduated from that school also.

Dad told me that he was a late bloomer in school, but that was because he spent time in the Navy, which gave him time to mature before he enlisted in Fordham University. He said that when he began college he had a thirst to learn every thing he could and his marks were far superior to his high school report cards, which he said were dismal.

Maturity makes a big difference when you are of schooling age. Those with sky high IQ's will often breeze through school effortlessly, but is seems to me that extra year or two is of great benefit as you trod, then trot in school. That's what Dad often said, and in my case he was right. I'm talking about the average student. I went from a no-student, to average student, to good student.

On the first day Dad dragged me to school I would have said thirty-five was a good age to start.

My next step was a special television school for a year where I learned the intricacies of TV. That enabled me to get a job at CBS, which made my father very happy. He wasn't happy that I was at CBS, just that I was progressing in life.

◆　◆　◆

At just about this time Mom decided we would move to Tucson, Arizona, where a friend of hers had just moved with her family. I knew their family well, often taking care of their kids. But the change from living in New York to living in Tucson is a whole new ball game.

The heat is dry, but it's still HEAT. Slow down I told myself in the beginning, but, of course, it's a gradual process. My father kept warning me of skin cancer, because of the intense sun in Arizona. So what happened? He got skin cancer in New York!

After Dad tells about "Life with Children," I'll break down the hyperboles and fill in some convenient tall tales, or at least stretches, that my literate father may very well have included in his tales. I'll have to read what he says first!

Wow! I just read it all. He never told me all those stories. He did take us all to Puerto Rico while he was working on the Wendy Barrie debacle. Yes, I said debacle.

He wouldn't let us see the rehearsals, or see the play itself, but I can read. I read the newspaper, San Juan Star, the next day. What a review! I think his worst enemy wrote it. I haven't read a review that bad till this day. O.K. I exaggerate. But not much.

And that quick reference to the girl I brought to New York. I really just glanced at it and didn't give it much thought. This business he writes about my bringing the pleasant girl from Tucson to New York to stay at his house with me. Unfortunately it's all true.

Talk about charm. When he took us out to lunch he was Cary Grant and George Clooney combined. That's my job! The girl wasn't supposed to be impressed with him. She was supposed to be impressed with me. Maybe I'm too touchy. Females were always attracted to Dad. I guess I'm a little jealous. O.K., more than a little.

The young lady and I (no name mentioned) saw New York, a first for her, and she was more impressed with "Our Town" than with Cary, George and me. As I read this I feel I'm being too hard on Dad. He was just being himself. No more no less.

Perhaps it was my amazement at his energy. I know my sister inherited a thirst to achieve. The fellow she married, Ricky Stack, doubles the whole O'Farrell clan in achievement. He's a real go-getter with a knack of drawing people to him and convincing them of whatever he's about. Ricky is a lot like Dad, blonde, talkative, energetic, and an achiever. Also nice looking but not as good-looking as any O'Farrell, and I'm not biased. Only a little.

On the other hand, I'm a layback fellow. I prefer to be quiet, observe and analyze those with whom I come in contact. Some people think I'm too quiet, but I don't feel the need to have others analyze me, or wonder what I'm thinking. Actually most people are so wrapped up with what they're doing or saying, they don't pay much attention to others. Self-absorbed I am not, and I'm thankful I'm that way.

It's not that I don't contribute. It's just that most others aren't that interested much in what you have to add. I like it like that. I take in the whole nine yards, and make friends easily. I'm the kind of guy who listens to them and chooses who is interesting and who is not. I hang out with the interesting ones.

Remember the fifth wall. That's me, and I know the other four walls by heart. I'm way ahead of the game of life. How comfortable! No vanity. Autographs upon request.

A perfect example would be the day my excitable father took me out to the racetrack. It was my first time at gambler's heaven, and my father drove faster than any of the horses ever ran in their lives.

As he finally found a parking space not too far from the grandstand at Belmont, the nicest track in New York, he said to me, "Hurry up, we have to make the first race. It begins in five minutes." With that, he slammed the car door, began running, stopped short and yelled, "Oh my God!"

With my usual equanimity I said nothing, but I knew the reason for Dad's explosion.

"I left the key in the car," he screamed.

"Not only that," I quietly whispered in his ear, "You also left the motor running." I was a teen-ager and didn't want to one-up my own father, but we quiet ones often take in more than we are given credit for.

When he slammed his car door after I had gotten out and I still heard the motor running, I knew we had a problem.

No use in saying something like, "Hey, Dumb-Dumb, when you stop the car you do it by turning the key to the off position, taking it out of its slot, placing it in your pocket, lock the door, close it, and hurry on your way. It's really quite simple and I am thirteen years old, but I don't want to seem out of place by telling you how to do something you've done a hundred times previously."

Something like that only would have fed the senior's exasperation.

"What do I do now?" He walked up and down completely perplexed.

I waited what I thought was a suitable amount of time and calmly suggested, "A place as large as this must have mechanics to help out. Seems reasonable."

His exhortations and my calm may have seemed like I was indifferent, but I was just hoping patiently for the volcanic Mauna Loa in Hawaii, in the form of my father, to finish his explosion.

"What a great idea," he said, as though I had discovered the Quark or perhaps another planet in the universe.

"Jim, you're a genius," he smiled at me.

It felt good, but I realized it was just logical thinking once you realized you would not get to the betting window in time to lose your money betting on the first race.

He disappeared, leaving me in charge of a running car, which was standing still because it was in the "park" position.

The son of a gun came running back with a mechanic and I realized he was hustling the racetrack employee to "hurry it up, hurry it up," as he waved a ten dollar bill over his head.

Humorous as this was for me, sadness encompassed the whole incident. I know my father was ecstatic at the idea of taking me out to the racetrack for the first time in my life. He was introducing me to a part of his life that he loved. And he really fouled up before he could get it started. In the most unimaginable way.

I think I helped out again later. I told him to place a bet on a horse whose name I liked, always a no-no with hard-core bettors. The horse won, and Big Jim collected eighteen dollars. This would cover all our costs, and he gave me a "fin," that's five dollars for us touts.

It was days like this that made life enjoyable. I felt like a real adult keeping my cool about the parked "running" car, while my adult companion was running around like a wounded warrior.

And picking out a winning horse in a close horserace. It gives you a thrill that runs up and down your back. It makes you forget the four other names you threw out in four other races, all of which ran like turtles. As long as you picked out a winner, the losers never happened. They never existed. They were ephemeral, but the winner was a lasting event. Particularly when you gave it to your Dad.

Shortly after, perhaps a few years later, we brought a super eight camera out to the track and took pictures of the greatest horse of all-time, Secretariat, romping home easily. And we parked the car with gentility.

◆　◆　◆

Now, before I continue with my overwhelmingly interesting life, I really have to straighten out this business about bringing my Tucson female friend to New York.

Dad and his wife Maria accepted us graciously, and I set out to be a perfect host to my good friend whom I'll call Alice, in as much as she may prefer to remain anonymous.

We went to the top of the Empire State building, and no we didn't see Meg Ryan, Deborah Kerr or hear music from "An Affair to Remember." We did see an absolutely breathtaking view of the grandeur of New York, and I was as thrilled as Alice, though I tried to be less than breathless about a montage that stirs the soul. I'm practiced about being blasé, but I really had to work to keep my own thrills under wraps. As the British would say if asked if this site isn't a brilliant spectacle, "Quite."

It was late that day and Maria had prepared a Veal Parmigiana ravished by all, and, after dinner, engaged Alice in friendly chitchat.

I must say Alice was ever so polite as she listened to all of us, but she began to take on the attributes of my famous "fifth" wall.

It dawned on me that perhaps she wasn't quite as literate or regal as I first thought. I don't expect Emily Dickinson or Hillary Clinton to be my companion, or someone in-between, but the Veal Parmigiana became the most interesting part of the evening.

I think Dad noticed this too, because as the lulls became more frequent and pronounced, he tried to light up the evening by telling us that tomorrow for lunch he was taking us to the, "absolute best restaurant in Westchester County." Seems that evening had a Parmigiana flavor right up to bedtime.

The next day at noon we drove to one of his special restaurants. Then it began. The Clooney-Grant charm.

I was hoping he wouldn't tell "The Story," the one that embarrassed me to death, the one he loved to tell even on subways to perfect strangers. But he did. It goes like this, Dad talking of course.

"You know, when Jim Jr. was little I received a letter from a boxing friend of mine, Jimmy Egan. Actually it was a solicitation for a donation to Jimmy Egan's campaign for Mayor of Pompton Lakes."

"I immediately called him and said, 'Egan, never mind money, I'll get Joe Louis to come out and campaign for you on the Saturday afternoon before the election'."

"You can get Joe Louis to come here?"

"I reminded him, 'Pompton Lakes was the place where he trained for some of his fights. When people hear Pompton Lakes, they think of Joe Louis. It's a natural'."

"Can you get him?"

"Relax," I assured him. "I'll have Louis there and you set up a celebration," was my reply. "Make it Joe Louis day." We agreed on the date, the Saturday I mentioned, and I immediately set to work.

Joe was living in a hotel a block off Central Park, and I called him and talked him and his wife into driving, or rather his chauffer driving, on the declared Saturday out to Pompton Lakes, New Jersey to campaign.

I told little Jim I was going to have him meet Joe Louis, and come along for the adventure. My son was about as impressed as a ten year old would be, which was so-so, but better than meeting a famous ping-pong player.

The appointed Saturday we drove to the Champion's hotel, entered his room as he let us in, and greeted us with more enthusiasm than that for which he was generally known. In fact, Joe Louis seemed to be having fun fooling around with little Jim before we finally left.

The trip was about forty-five minutes, and at the entry to the town we met the Chief of Police whom we had telephone upon leaving.

This chief was the happiest law officer in America; because he had been Louis' early morning roadwork companion for all of Joe's big fights and hadn't seen the Champ since.

They embraced as long lost brothers, and the chief escorted Joe and Mrs. Louis into a beautiful convertible with a sign across the trunk welcoming the great fighter. The sign said, 'Welcome Home Joe', and a band was lined up in front of the car ready to march and play stirring music.

A whistle was blown and the festivities began as hundreds of people lined the streets and waved and yelled. Joe grinned ear to ear, and the Chief of Police looked like he had just entered heaven.

They both waved and smiled back and Jim and I, in my car, directly followed the celebrities, as Louis' chauffer followed me.

I was so excited at the great spectacle of a hometown hero returning, I began to wave also. Little Jim put his hand on my shoulder as if to say enough, already. I got the message and quieted down.

When we were midway into town the mini-caravan stopped. A table had been set up with a microphone and loads of pens, and we left our cars.

The chief made a very gracious speech and announced that the 'Brown Bomber' as Louis was affectionately known, would be signing autographs for all the children in the town.

I stood next to Jimmy Egan, who was next to Louis and asked, "Where is the photographer?"

"What photographer?"

'Didn't you arrange to have a newspaper photographer take a picture of you two shaking hands and kissing each other. Your opponent for Mayor has to be going crazy thinking of tomorrow's paper, front-page picture of Joe Louis endorsing you. You couldn't buy that kind of publicity.'

"Egan gave us an Aw Shucks look and said, 'Everybody knows I brought him here.'"

'I wanted to die. How dumb can one person be? I guess it wasn't being dumb, just shyness. I wasn't going to argue the point, as all the kids were lining up in front of the autograph table. There had to be a hundred or more young ones, and they all seemed to have their own pencils and papers.'

'At exactly that moment I started to say something to my little Jim, but he wasn't there. I looked around, but no Jim. I became frantic. He had disappeared. Maybe he was searching for a bathroom. Now, I was searching for him.'

'After five minutes of utter frustration, I spotted him. *He was standing at the back of the autograph line with a pencil in his hand! Half a block away.*'

Alice was intently listening. She leaned forward in her chair. Her eyes were fixed on Dad and occasionally she glanced at me, but she didn't say a word. She wanted to hear the end of the story. Dad continued.

"What are you doing here?" I questioned.

'That's Joe Louis!' Jim pointed, as though he had never seen him before, nor shook his hand in the hotel room, nor joked together before we left the hotel.

And then it hit me. It was all meaningless, their meeting, joking, the ride to Pompton Lakes, the band, the Police Chief, until…all the other kids wanted an autograph. Then, and only then, was Joe Louis a figure larger than life, the greatest fighter the world had ever known. A figure that every teenager and adult throughout the world would walk miles to be proud owners of his autograph.

'And he, Jimmy O'Farrell had visited Joe in Louis's hotel room, spent time with him and just a few other adults.'

'It took the adulation and excitement of all the other kids his age for it all to sink in. Jim was now special.'

◆　◆　◆

Dad had really laid it on.

Alice realized the story ended. She said nothing for a pregnant moment. She started to speak, then stopped. Finally, she looked at me and slowly said, "Who is Joe Louis?"

Later, after the lunch when we got home and I was alone with Dad, he said to me, "She never heard of Joe Louis."

I ruefully nodded.

"Get rid of her, Jim. Remember about the hobgoblins of little minds."

When we got back to Tucson, I did, as politely as I possibly could. She probably never heard of Hitler.

In the meantime, Jimmy Egan lost his run for Mayor by forty five votes, votes which he might have picked up had those forty five people seen the Champ holding Egan's hand high in premature victory, as those voters enjoyed their breakfasts while reading the morning newspapers.

One picture in a newspaper is almost as good as a television speech. People are tiring of the vacuous words sported by politicos, and a picture plants a memory, particularly one as famous as Joe Louis standing next to you in approbation. I heard Dad talking to Egan before we left to go back home.

"I slipped him a hundred dollar bill when we shook hands," he was telling his buddy in hushed tones, but I caught the gist. "Louis really appreciated it."

When we were driving home I could see Dad was in less than a joyous mood. He drove without saying anything. This was not my father's M.O. He started mumbling to himself. As the car sped faster and faster, my father let out this vocal arrangement, not too dissimilar to Don Quixote's songs in *The Man of La Mancha.*

"One photographer, One lousy photographer, One freaking photographer" and he was singing this at the top of his vocal chords.

"We had the impossible dream," he roared, less and less on key. Dulcet he was not. Finally, he reverted to his normal talking voice and changed back to being my Dad, Don Quixote out the window now.

"That dumb, stupid Irishman. All we needed was one photograph, one photograph, and it cost me a hundred bucks."

I slickly said to him, "I thought this was all about me meeting Joe Louis."

Daddy looked at me, turned the wheel to follow the road, then looked back at me. He thought a long moment.

"You know, Son," he said in a quiet voice. "You're right. That's why I went through this whole thing. I wanted to be a big shot in the eyes of my son. Did I make it?" At that moment I adored him.

"You bet you did." Then we both started singing *The Impossible Dream.* When we finished together we laughed all the way back home.

It was a day I'll never forget. It will always be in my treasure chest of memories.

◆   ◆   ◆

My days now at the University of Arizona will never be as exciting as the days in New York. I go occasionally to Mexico, an hour or so away. Sometimes with friends, sometimes alone. It's fun, but not exciting.

I go to the James Bond conventions in California and mingle with the stars, but I'm not a kid, and I realize we're all pretty much equals.

I do admit I've always been a James Bond Groupie, and some of the kid excitement is resurrected, but it's ephemeral.

I return from the conventions to the home in Arizona where I live alone. Mom died just a few years after we arrived in Tucson. I think I can stand loneliness better than most people. I disc jockey as a sideline and do this and that. I am not garrulous, consequently, I have many friends.

But, *I'll never be a kid again*. And that hurts most of all.

My Sister's Tale—Anne Marie

If these two Neanderthals think they can tell the world about their various and sundry adventures without letting me squeeze through their male made world, they had better get their screwdrivers out and tighten the screws in their heads.

I was first-born child and hereby declare "primus adventurous," my brother Jim, "secundus adventurous" was born four years after me, and has always been four years "de minimus." Let him look all that up in the dictionary. I don't like to brag, I really don't, but I've always been better looking, classier, and smarter.

If it weren't for me his I.Q. would be halved. It was I who brought him to school every morning, Mom and Dad being teachers in schools at a great distance from our house, and Jim's school only a few blocks from mine. Did I say, "brought" him? How about dragged him? Threatened him? What a nudge!

Little Jim learned from me, particularly how to handle Dad. One day I misbehaved and Dad gave me a whack on my fanny. Tears rolled down my eyes and Daddy stood there looking as if he wanted to go to confession. What a sucker. Every time after I thought my fanny was going to get its due I got the tears welling up, which brought out the premature guilt on my father's face and a stern lecture. A lot better than a whack! Poor guy, I had him pegged and he won't know it till he reads this. Sorry Dad, but one does have to save her derriere.

I think the best times in my life were when Daddy brought me downtown to see Broadway shows. He produced shows himself, but there was nothing like Broadway. After we saw "Oliver" we were standing outside the theatre for quite a while (I don't remember why) and the young star came out with his mother. I wanted to tell Dad to get his autograph, but that would have been too forward. My father didn't pay much attention, but I was in love for five minutes.

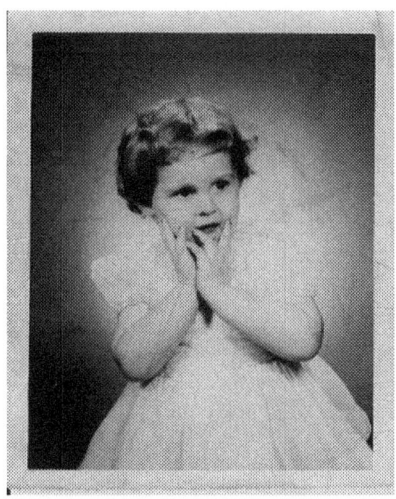

Oooh, you want me to be an actress?

It wasn't so bad. I'd rather produce.

When I asked my father's opinion he proclaimed the young star an 88 for looks. I argued that he was a 98. We weren't talking in code, just one of my father's many peculiarities, although obsessions would be closest to the truth! It seems Daddy gives everything a number. He can swear it's a quirky carryover from his teaching career, but don't you think it would have stopped by this time?

I can ask him if he thinks it will rain tomorrow and he will pause awhile and finally answer, "46." He measures everything in his own numerical classification, and we all understand. I will ask, "What did you think of Mr. Jones at last night's party, the man who was telling the jokes that had us all laughing hysterically?" "23," will be his answer, meaning poor Jones flunked. He didn't reach a 65, which is Dad's passing mark, and also the passing mark he used for his English and Drama classes when he was teaching.

His wife, Maria, was a student of his in the 7th grade class, and he never gave her higher than an 85, which is close to Heaven in his estimation, but not hers. He has since told me she's a 95 as a wife. I don't think he'd give God 100.

He has a new telephone which gives the name of the person calling before he picks it up. I expect one day, when he sees my name, or Jimmy's name, he will pick up the phone and yell out, "100," before he says, "Hello." Obviously he is always thrilled when we call him. At that point I will tell him he is totally obsessed, not peculiar. He contains this idiosyncrasy only for our immediate family, knowing full well those men in the white jackets will take him away if he expands it to the public at large.

I still say young Oliver was a 98. We left and I had to find another star to fall in love with. Couldn't find one that age.

I hope my husband, Rick, doesn't get jealous. We've produced seven or eight shows together since then, and none of my stars can hold a candle to that little Oliver. What a doll he was.

But this is jumping ahead. My next love was Rudyard Kipling. I never heard of him until my father introduced him to me.

Seems my brother, Jim, and I had been begging for a dog. My father said we could have a dog under two conditions. One, my brother and I had to alternate taking him out. Two, his name had to be Rudyard Kipling, my father's favorite author. We agreed without hesitation, and a lovely poodle soon adorned our household. You don't think we upheld our part of the bargain, do you? Daddy ended up taking the dog out half the time, and we called him "Kippy."

One night Dad took him out. Kippy broke away from the leash and headed for Afghanistan. I'm sure he missed the mountains and the poetry. They say writers have to write. Of course we never asked for another dog. Kippy never even left us a poem. Just pleasant memories. Dad swears Kippy broke away from his leash, and there is no reason not to believe him, except our father is more than capable of extreme measures. Just kidding Dad,…more or less. We know you loved Kippy as much as we did. Come to think of it you played with the poodle more than you played with us. Huh!

◆ ◆ ◆

As we grew older we moved from the Bronx to a complex in Whitestone, Long Island called Le Havre. We needed another room, as Jimmy and I used the same bedroom in the Bronx and now in Long Island we each had our own room in this larger apartment.

I missed my friends from our previous location, but it didn't take long to meet new friends at Bayside High, where I was now at school. Dad always quoted a saying he had heard, and how well it fit. "Teen age girls are like wild horses with their manes flying in the wind." The girls at high school made the wild horses look tame.

Their main courses were boys. All the scholarly necessities such as Math, Science, et. al. lagged a distant second, third and as far back as the eye could see. Yet, the girls managed good marks, quite often better than the boys. I guess that may have been because so many of the boys majored in girls. The sexes finally met, face-to-face, etc. The etc. covers a lot of ground. I can see you all smiling as you think back. Hey, it was lots of fun. Painful at times for some, but fun for many others.

For me it was more fun than pain, but all life is a combination of both, something everyone experiences with time.

◆ ◆ ◆

The toughest pain for me was when my father left. Even though he telephoned every night and came over on weekends, emptiness filled the house and everything changed. Dad was a strict father, but one you could usually get around, one way or another.

My mother couldn't hold the reins as tightly as my father, even though she tried mightily. Perhaps it was his physical presence; maybe the fact that there were always his friends, such as the professional fighters, in the house, the fighters whom Dad trained and managed. That was to be no more. It emphasized the emptiness. The fighters were always sweet to Jimmy and me. Dad often said that people had a misimpression of boxers. He said they were able to get the hostility out of themselves by training in the gym, hitting what he called the "sand bag" for two or three rounds and sparring in the ring. Many times he told us fighters were exhausted every day after their workouts and didn't want any more physical conflict for the rest of the day.

Every once in a while we would read of a fighter like Jake LaMotta, a champion, getting in trouble, but that was an aberration. He said fighters were sweet guys outside the ring and Jimmy and I found that to be true, judging from the pugilists that so often came to our home in the Bronx. Dad was always complaining that people saw rough, tough guys fighting in the ring and assumed they were that way outside the ring.

He used Rocky Marciano as an example. He and Rocky trained together and were friends outside the gym, often dining together, and he told us Rocky was the gentlest man he ever met. Yet Rocky would brutalize his opponent in the ring.

The few times we would all watch a fight on television Dad would make us notice how the two warriors would hug each other after the final bell rang. You would think they were long lost brothers who had just met after years of separation, instead of two strangers who had been pounding away at each other until the last second of the battle.

Dad pointed out many things about people, their actions and reactions. I would say he was "people conscious" and we learned so much. Maybe that's why he became a teacher.

I often thought I might teach, but my life took a different track. I started college at the age of sixteen. I was really too young, emotionally and intellectually unprepared. Even though my marks were good in high school I just wasn't ready to compete with older students, and I dropped out of school after the first term.

I thought getting away from all the unhappiness would solve my problems, so I took off for California with two girl friends. Changing locales rarely helps your problems, so after four months we all decided to return back home to Long Island.

After returning, I worked at various "nowhere" jobs, but I was once again with Mom and Jimmy. I was back in New York where I felt I fit. California may be fine for others, but it was not for me.

Three years of being a waitress and trying sundry other jobs didn't prepare me for any profession, but it did mature me emotionally, and at the age of nineteen I was ready to hit the books and give college another try.

I registered at Queens College and majored in Drama. I now felt comfortable and I know other students looked up to me, as I was older than they. In drama class we went through many things Dad had taught me when I was young, such as improvisation and pantomime, so I was ready when our acting class was called upon to put on a play. The play was to be the classic *Our Town*.

We tried out for different parts, each student hoping to be the lead, some classmates hoping to just get a role, any role.

After the try-outs the professor took aside the students he had chosen and told them what part they would have and what he expected of them and how they should approach their roles.

He called my name and I was ecstatic. I approached him with great joy and asked him with unbearable apprehension what role I would have. He looked at me in a very matter of fact manner and said, "Anne Marie, you will be the prostitute."

"What?" I roared vehemently. "Why do I get that role?"

Now he was taken back at my reaction. He thought quickly and gave me his life saving answer. "Because you're the prettiest girl in the class and that will make the role believable."

I had heard enough cons in my life having lived with an Irish brother and father for many years not to recognize con, even if it was coming from a drama professor, so I marched back to my seat before he could tell me how to prepare for the role.

The play was a huge success and I guess my acting was O.K., even if I was the most depressed prostitute in the history of civilization.

◆ ◆ ◆

I graduated with a B.A. in drama and put acting behind me.

Love did come into my life, though. A blondish, medium height, cute, energetic fellow about my age often came around to where fellows and girls hung out and attracted the attention of quite a few females.

His name was Ricky Stack, and, in my opinion, he was arguably the most attractive of males I had ever come across. His sense of humor, and his constant probing of intellectual subjects beyond the grasp of most of the other girls put him head and shoulders above the other fellows with whom we engaged.

He loved sports and when he was with the guys he'd shoot baskets on the playgrounds. He seemed to be all things to all people, and he certainly became all things to me.

Anne Marie Stack I often daydreamed. But I knew I wouldn't give up my last name O'Farrell. Stubborn Irish you know. Anyhow, after all sorts of feminine deceits, Ricky and I decided to live together. We found an apartment in Manhattan, a walk up with a little garden in the back.

Ricky, with his flair for attracting people to his side, talked a fellow who was running an adult learning center in Manhattan into giving him fifty percent of the center in exchange for his ideas and full time work improving the enrollment of the center, which was doing poorly at that time.

Everything improved at the learning center many fold, and when the original owner left, our fifty percent was worth more than you can imagine. All the new courses Rick had initiated were over crowded and other courses were booming. He even got Phil Jackson, the basketball star of the Knicks, to work for us, teaching basketball courses at gymnasiums throughout the city. Phil, retired from the Knicks at the time, was in between gigs and hadn't yet signed on with the Los Angeles Lakers, so having him work for us was a big highlight for the school.

We re-named the school *Westwinds* and our fortunes were flying high. Enrollment was excellent and we were making a reputation.

Finally we received an offer to sell Westwinds for enough to insure a few years of traveling, getting married and starting new ventures. I had complete faith that Rick would come up with something. He was constantly going to sessions of Jane Roberts, well known psychic, whose primary teachings included "creating your own reality," and "there are no accidents in life." Rick was devoted to this philosophy and made things happen because he firmly believed and carried through his beliefs.

I went to many of Jane Roberts' classes where she was in contact with Seth. Seth was an out of body entity, a spirit guide, who spoke through Jane and imparted the philosophy encompassing a variety of life affirming realities. Rick put everything he learned from Jane Roberts into effect and we were now in a great financial position.

We made our first vacation upstate to New Paltz. There we were married. I still kept my name, Anne Marie O'Farrell.

We traveled to Japan, Singapore, Tahiti, Hong Kong, Thailand and Europe. Beautiful, interesting and educational, but time to get back to the states and begin another entrepreneurship. I brought back a red robe made in Hong Kong for my father. He loved it.

◆ ◆ ◆

Seventy Eighth Street and Columbus Ave was fine for us, but not Cody. Cody was a newcomer growing in my body, forming, developing and telling us by a series of kicks, now and again, that we would be a threesome when he was ready to make his entrance into this world.

He decided to make his appearance in May, choosing of course, the month celebrated in honor of mothers. That meant we would both take our bows in the same month. What a ham. He may be a Stack, but O'Farrell blood was still in him. From then on I would have to share my month with him. That's like upstaging a fellow thespian in an important show. Oh well!

Mid-Manhattan worried me as a place to bring up a newborn. Heavy traffic, hustle and bustle did not seem ideal for a little guy running around with abandon, so I talked Ricky into searching Long Island for a new home where we could now have peace and quiet. I felt Columbus Ave was the tops for a twosome, but not for the three of us.

My husband found a lovely house in Manhasset, and in short order we moved in. Our funds, however, were being depleted, so Rick came up with the idea of producing shows. He had no background in theater, and I was limited to a degree in Drama. My thoughts immediately went to my father's difficulties in the Wendy Barrie epic, but my spouse convinced me that with his business acumen we would succeed. His Jane Roberts' "creating your own reality" philosophy was always his bible, and he lived by it.

Our first venture was in the basement of a Sterns department store close to our new house. *Café Noir* was the name of the play and Dad helped by giving tips to the actors and actresses. Pops was a good acting teacher.

The play was a limited success, but it would not be enough to carry us for any length of time. We had formed a corporation called New Awareness Network, and now we had to expand into other venues. An Off Broadway show called *Joey & Mary's Irish Italian Comedy Wedding* was the current rage and we thought the format would really take off. It did. We produced our own inter-active shows written by Rick and other writers. My hubby also managed to write a book *Out of Body Adventures* an offshoot of Seth (the Jane Roberts spirit guide) material, which has been praised worldwide.

We produce special shows for corporations and organizations that request entertainment for their employees and members, usually during the holidays. These are very profitable and augment the gross we make throughout the year in our regular shows, such as *The Soapranos* and *The Honeymoaners* to name a few. I have enjoyed the excitement of developing and opening a new show, but it has not been without the pain that accompanies the joy.

Above all, I often feel crushed when we are having tryouts for a new show. Turning down the actors and actresses who are trying out for different parts and sending them home with sentences like "Thank you, we'll contact you if you get the part" is just a polite way of saying "no" and crushing their hopes of being chosen. It is almost as painful to me as it is to them, as they leave the audition room with faces crestfallen and almost hopeless. So many of them have been turned down repeatedly, and with each "no" is a measure of pain. It makes me realize that my being chosen as the prostitute in *Our Town* in college was a plus, not a minus. At least I was chosen. Rejection is such a bitter pill, particularly when it happens repeatedly and oh so personally.

Thankfully, when we have produced shows in other cities, Detroit, Philadelphia, et. al. I have not gone along and I don't have to go through the try-out process, choosing this one and slamming the door on another one, no matter how politely.

◆　◆　◆

One summer we decided we would mix business with pleasure and go to Saratoga, New York. Saratoga is renowned for its resort specialties, such as a spa, a racetrack and great hotels among other things. The idea of hotels putting on shows for business organizations had been growing in leaps and bounds as we found out when we booked our shows in different cities. They were very profitable. Our show would be booked into the restaurant of a hotel, and the hotel would earn its profit from the money we would give it from the charge the customer paid for a meal and our production. Everyone was happy with this arrangement, particularly the customer.

This was our first trip to Saratoga, and, if we were unable to work out a deal, at least we would be able to have an enjoyable part to our summer, taking in the sights, relaxing to some extent and enjoying the beauty of one of the countries greatest resorts.

We brought Cody with us, as he was off from school, and checked into a hotel we thought might be interested in one of our productions. Also, this would enable Rick to check the prices at this particular place and, if not feasible here, he could check other hotels to see if they might be interested in our deal. Poor Rick didn't get the physical rest Cody and I did, but we acted as consultants, which meant at night we would go over the costs of a production, the cost we would be able to charge an organization, the amount certain hotel restaurants would demand for dinners, and the profit we would be able to earn after all expenses were paid.

The first night we were very tired after the long drive from Long Island. We decided we would have dinner in a particular hotel's restaurant and then watch some television. As we ordered I chatted with the waitress.

"Have you heard?" she asked.

"Heard what?" I responded.

"Robert Redford is staying here in our hotel. He's producing a movie and is looking at Saratoga as a location for one of his scenes," she answered.

We all looked at each other with surprise, amazement, and joy. How exciting. Here we were, small time producers staying at the same hotel as one of America's biggest stars and producers. The rest of our dinner conversation was filled with Robert Redford talk; his roles in his movies, his productions and general appreciation for his work as an actor, actor/producer and just about everything he had ever done.

"I hope we get a chance to see him while we're here," Cody said. That was one thing we all agreed upon.

The next morning before we left our room for breakfast I told Rick I'd go down to the paper stand in the lobby and bring up some of the day's newspapers. Rick and Cody had barely arisen and had not yet showered or dressed. I was out the door before anyone could tell me anything about buying the papers later. It was obvious what I wanted. I could buy the papers; sit on the lobby sofa apparently reading the paper, but only with one eye. The other eye was peeled for Redford if, by chance, he would happen to cross the lobby. Then I could tell my clan I was the first to see the actor. I figured fifteen minutes of this newspaper loitering and I might bring home the trophy, the trophy, of course, being the first to come across the star.

It was a wasted fifteen minutes, as there was no sight of anyone of importance and I didn't get to read one page of *The New York Times*. When I returned to the room both males were busily getting ready for breakfast and paid no attention to me, the sports pages being the first thing they were interested in. I knew the odds were against me when I went out, but who knows, luck could have been a lady that morning.

◆ ◆ ◆

During the day, Rick checked out our hotel restaurant and other hotels as Cody and I walked around and saw the sights. After dinner, we went over the figures. It appeared any promotion we might undertake would be too costly and produce minimal profits. Expenses were just too high. It looked like a no-go.

We were lying around watching television and Rick opened a can of Coke he had brought back to the room.

"Honey, there's an ice machine down the hall. These Cokes aren't that cold. Would you go down the hall and get us some ice. There's an empty bucket on that table. You can fill it with ice. O.K.?"

My poor husband looked exhausted, and I took the bucket and headed for the door, "Get a lot of ice," he said. "Remember, there are three of us."

"Right," was my answer as I opened the door to do my master's bidding. Before I closed the door behind me the door directly across the hall opened. There he was a bucket in his hand too. Redford, *THE* Robert Redford was in the room opposite ours, and he was going to get ice also.

Oh my God, what do I do, what do I say? Do I run back and get my gang to gape. They were in their underwear. My brain went on vacation. My tongue went on vacation. I simply stared as he headed toward the ice machine. I hadn't nodded or said, "Hello," as the actor and I came out at exactly the same time.

I followed him brain dead, star struck. He finished getting his ice as I arrived, gave me a half nod as I stepped to the machine. He walked by me his head lowered as if trying not to be recognized. How could one of the most recognized, famous men in the world not be recognized?

I stood staring at the machine. Maybe he'd think I needed help and would come back and help me. Dream on Anne Marie dream on. I woke from my daze long enough to fill the ice bucket just as he was preparing to open his door.

"I saw you in…" "You were one of my favorite…" Nothing came out of my mouth, thank God. How many people have shouted just such simplicities at him in his lifetime. I'm glad I was not one of them, now.

I went back to my room.

"You won't believe…" I started.

"I know, you saw Robert Redford," Cody said.

Was my son psychic?

"We figured we'd tease you when you came back," Ricky laughed.

"No, no, I did, honest."

It took me half an hour to convince them of what really happened. Finally, when they realized I was telling the truth, not kidding, the questions started popping. "What did he look like, what did he say."

"He's smaller than he looks on screen, his face seemed to have some scars on it, and for what we talked about, well, some things a woman keeps to herself."

"Aw, Mom," Cody said.

"Here's your ice, now cool it. Our conversation will be between Robert and me." I picked up a newspaper and began reading it. "No more questions, please," was my lady-like retort. After they read this they'll know. Sorry fellows. I think Rick, knowing me pretty well, figured it out. Particularly when I said "Robert."

Saratoga didn't work out for us production wise. But I did have my little adventure, and we all had fun.

◆   ◆   ◆

Dad was overjoyed at our successes and bragged to all his friends to the point of bringing those friends to some of our productions. He always had that "my daughter and son-in-law are behind what you are seeing" look on his face. I knew he was proud, but he managed to keep it low-key. Our successes were so fruitful we were able to purchase a summer home in the Hamptons.

The reader has to realize that this was practically 24/7 work and never without problems. I actually got into a fight at one New Year's Eve show. I mean a fist-fight. Oh how I wish Daddy were there that night.

In these audience participation shows there is a bar for the audience, and they get their drinks between acts. What I always fear will happen, happened. After the second act in one show, two men who had been visiting the bar frequently between acts got into an argument. I don't know what they were arguing about (I hope it wasn't the show) but things became so heated between them that they began to throw punches at each other. Not very good punches, I must say. Wrestling also ensued. I looked around for my stage manager, but he was hiding.

All my childhood I watched my father teach his son how to throw left jabs and right crosses and all the other God forsaken things fighters do in the ring. Now it was my turn. But Dad never taught me! Anyhow, I went to where the brawl was taking place and threw a jab at somebody, I didn't know whom. Turned out it was one of my actors who was trying to break up the fight. My aim was always lousy. Fortunately he had a small role, and he finished the play with a fat lip. He was mumbling like Marlon Brando. I mean no disrespect to the great actor, but occasionally he did mumble.

My left hand was swollen for weeks. Damn Dad. He could have taught me too! My stage manager finally called the police and order was restored.

Jimmy never got in a fight in his life, and he knew how to fight. I threw one punch with my 120 pounds and almost broke my fist. Fate often gets things mixed up.

To this day Dad won't teach me how to fight, so I got my husband to teach me how to run. Whenever the next altercation comes up I will be the fastest person on the scene, with my feet. Girls aren't supposed to fight Daddy says, and my left hand agrees with him.

The fact is my father often kids me about being a "Cinderella Kid." I'm not interested. I want to be a Jesse Owens!

♦   ♦   ♦

Bad news came shortly after this event. Mom and Jim had moved Tucson, Arizona. Mom became very sick. I left for Tucson, but not too many days after I got there Mom died. It was another crushing blow.

Jimmy stayed there, but I returned after the funeral. To this day I think of the fights Mom and I had when I was young, and the love we shared after the fights.

Dad remarried. Her name is Maria, a wonderful human being whom Jimmy and I respect and have come to love.

I miss my mother so much, but Rick and I know she is watching us from elsewhere. We believe this with all our hearts and I have no doubt the successes we have had up to this time have been guided, at least in part, by a loving mother, as well as encouraged by a loving father.

My brother, huh. I still have a good right hand, Jimmy, and I could lick you when we were kids. Just remember that, next time you leave Tucson. I'm four years older than you and I've put on weight. I now weigh 126 pounds. Just in case, I can run like a deer.

Right Dad? If only you had taught me, the police wouldn't have had to stop those two drunks. I would have knocked them both out.

But that's okay. Let there be no ambiguity. I love you mucho.

The Final Curtain

In this book I have outlined the "Tales of my father, sister and myself, with the hope that the reader has, at the very least, a snapshot of a functional family in today's world.

We have taken each day with the hilarity and love the day offers, sharing our lives with the reader. We epitomize the good and the bad, but not the ugly. We refuse to recognize the ugly. Ugly is not a part of our vernacular.

Does the ugly exist? Of course it exists, if you allow it to diminish any part of your life. Many people carry the ugly with them, and, in so doing, instill deeper in their beings unfillable voids.

There is little sadness in the "Tales" of our trio. Disappointments, failures, successes and joys, described in an atmosphere of heightened reality, are meant to bring the reader along for the joyride on the carousel of life.

Life to us has never been the humdrum of sunrises and sunsets, work without play, existence without excitement.

Our "Tale" tellers regret not a moment, knowing there is always tomorrow.

I ask the reader to step up to our carousel of laughter and enjoyment and breathe the breathtaking moments which life provides daily.

I will reluctantly admit the fact that I'll "Never be a boy again," as I said in my "tale," but I've had a helluva life as a man.

About the Author

Jim O'Farrell Jr. is currently working as an analyst at the University of Arizona. He always promised himself that his first book would be about the vicissitudes of his family. He is currently working on a spy novel.

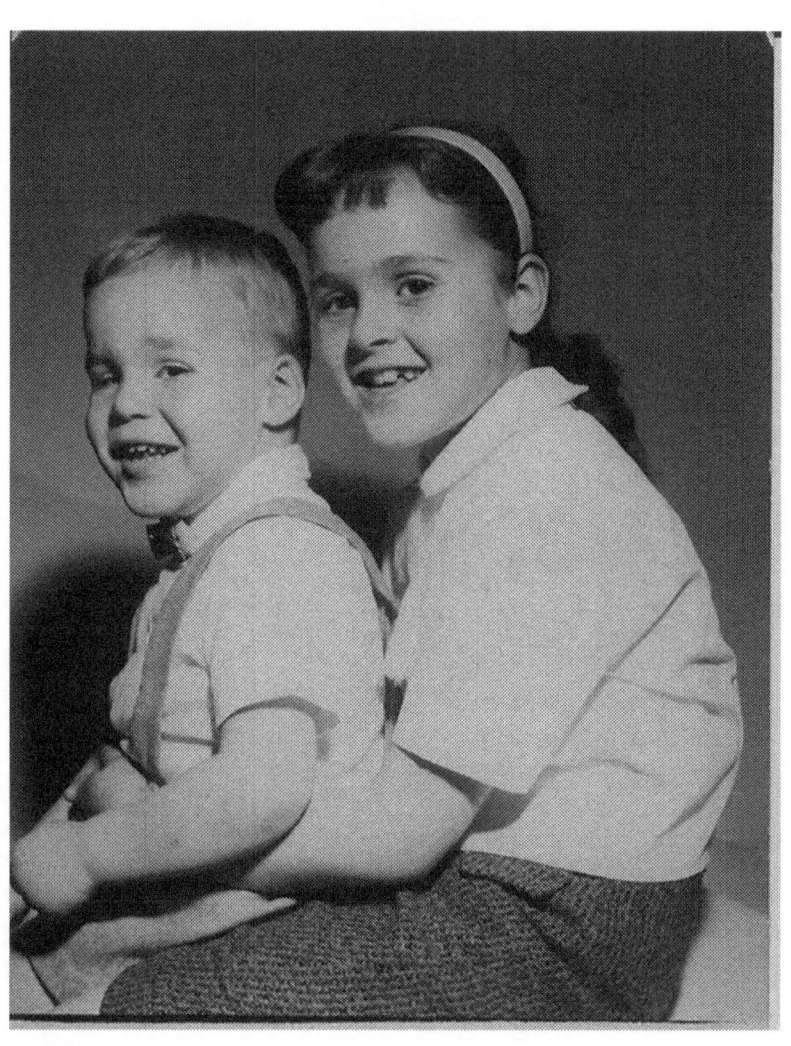

978-0-595-38442-6
0-595-38442-0